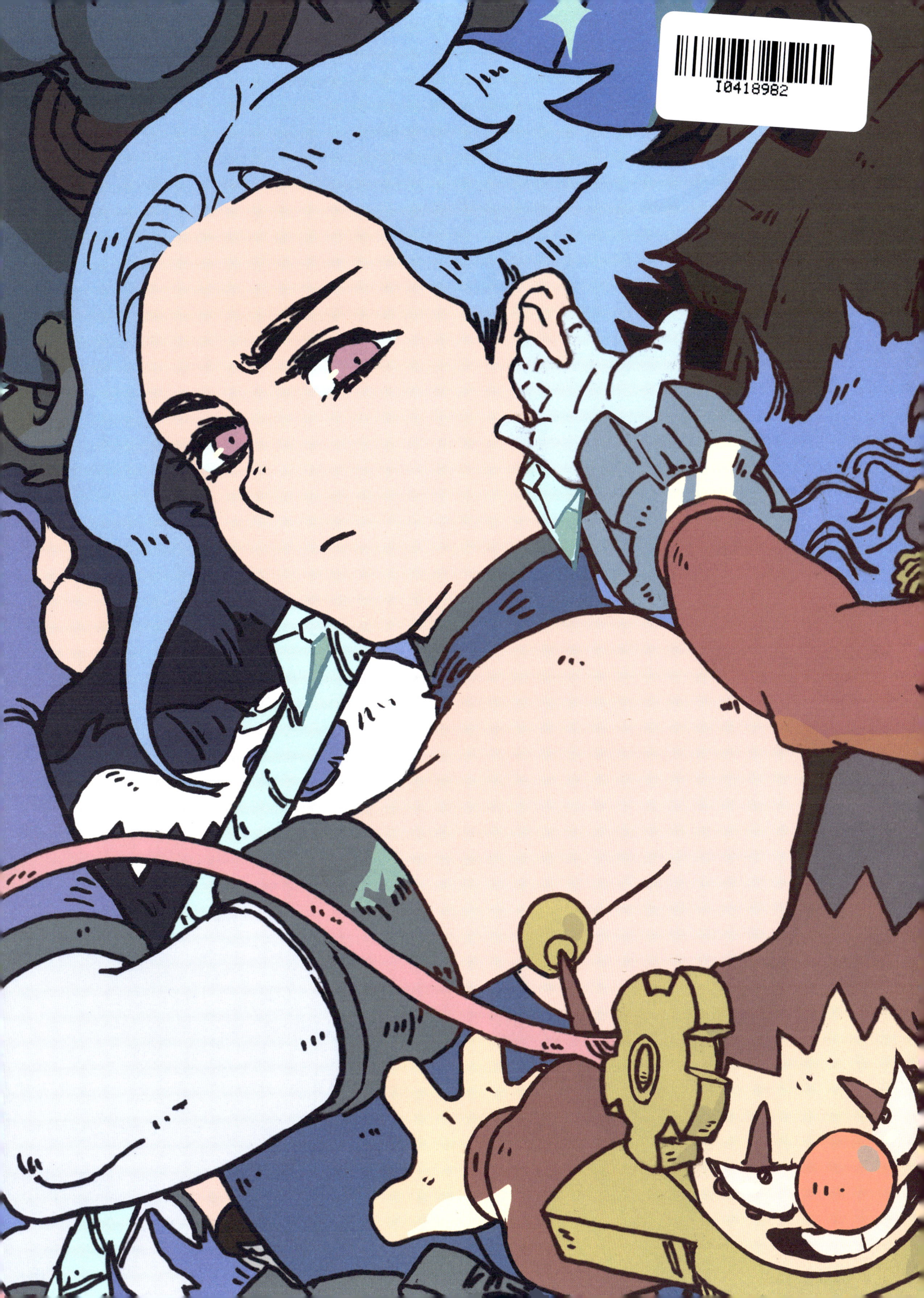

SABOTAGE

AN INDIE STUDIO
FROM QUEBEC CITY

EST. 2016

SEA OF STARS

THROES OF THE WATCHMAKER

PRESENT-DAY BRYCE:
Just like with the previous *Sea of Stars* art book, the commentary in this book is 90% taken from the Slack conversations between me and Thierry, the creative director of *Sea of Stars*, from December 2023 to January 2025.

We definitely settled into a rhythm after working together for so long. I also became a lot more descriptive, adventurous, and playful with what I was willing to pitch to Thierry. Personally, I feel like the work improved a lot as it continued forward and I hope you enjoy seeing the process!

Best,
Bryce Kho

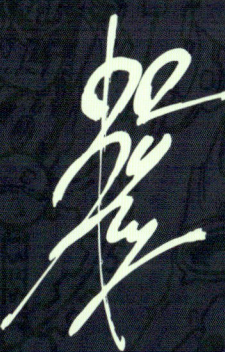

3dtotal Publishing

3dtotalPublishing

Correspondence: **publishing@3dtotal.com**

Website: **store.3dtotal.com**

First published in the United Kingdom, 2025, by 3dtotal Publishing.

Address: 3dtotal.com Ltd,
29 Foregate Street, Worcester,
WR1 1DS, United Kingdom.

Hard cover ISBN: 978-1-915992-37-6

Printed and bound in China by C&C Offset Printing Co., Ltd

Visit **store.3dtotal.com** for a complete list of available book titles.

Designer: Bryce Kho
Editorial Project Manager: Rhiannon Joseph
Lead Editor: Samantha Rigby
Lead Designer: Joseph Cartwright
Studio Manager: Simon Morse
Managing Director: Tom Greenway

FSC — MIX
Paper | Supporting responsible forestry
FSC® C008047

50%
of net profits donated
TO CHARITY

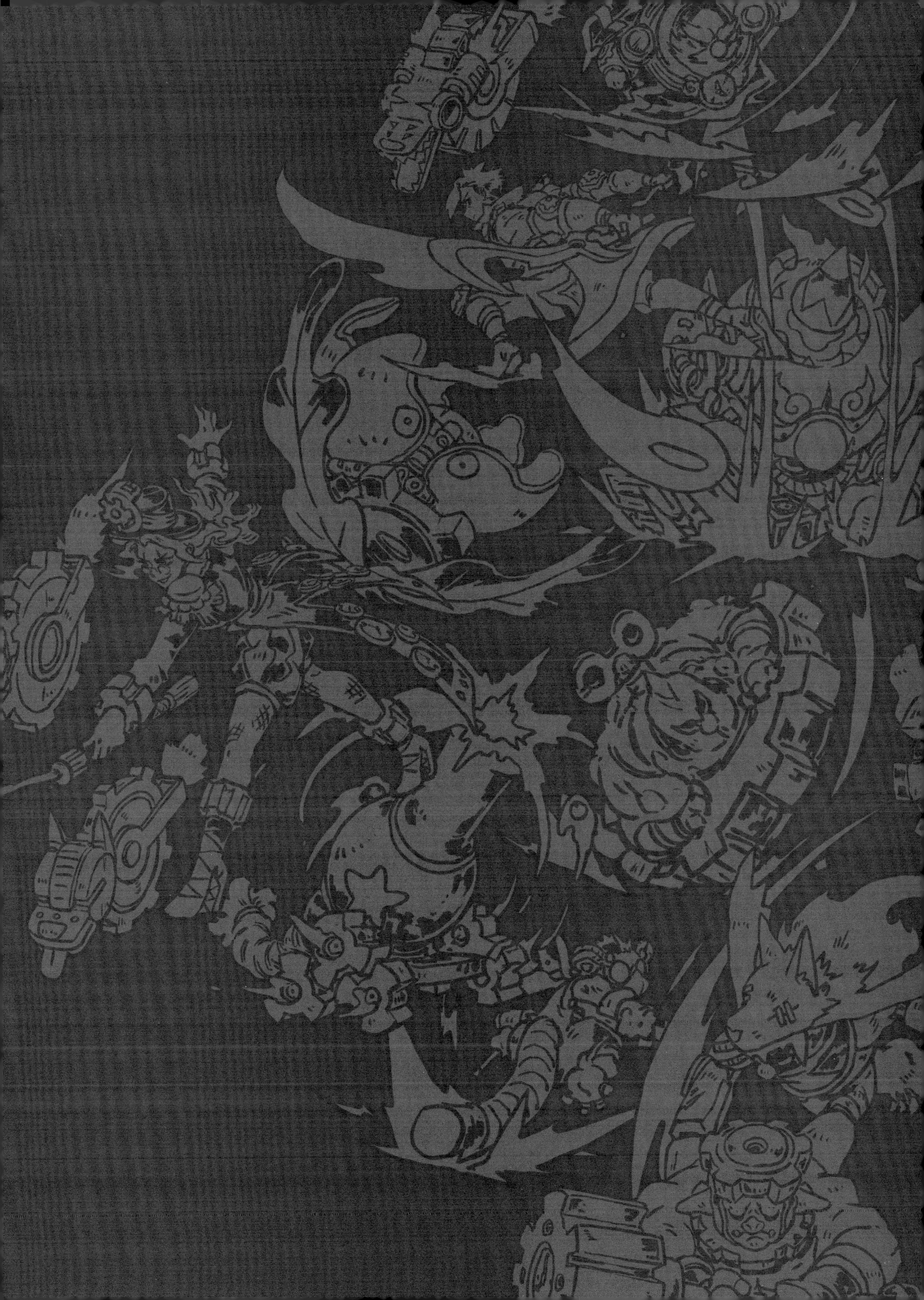

Pif & Pouf

THIERRY: First up, here are the two harlequin/clown twins. They are meant to be playful and evil, completing each other's sentences all the time in an over-the-top way that doesn't contribute much, such as 'It will be thoroughly fascinating, Pif!' and 'It will be haphazardly convoluting, Pouf!'

We'll also be giving them a bunch of overproduced talk animations where, instead of just their mouth moving, they do super-involved circus tricks that jump cut in and out without transition, like riding a unicycle, juggling, swallowing a sword, and so on.

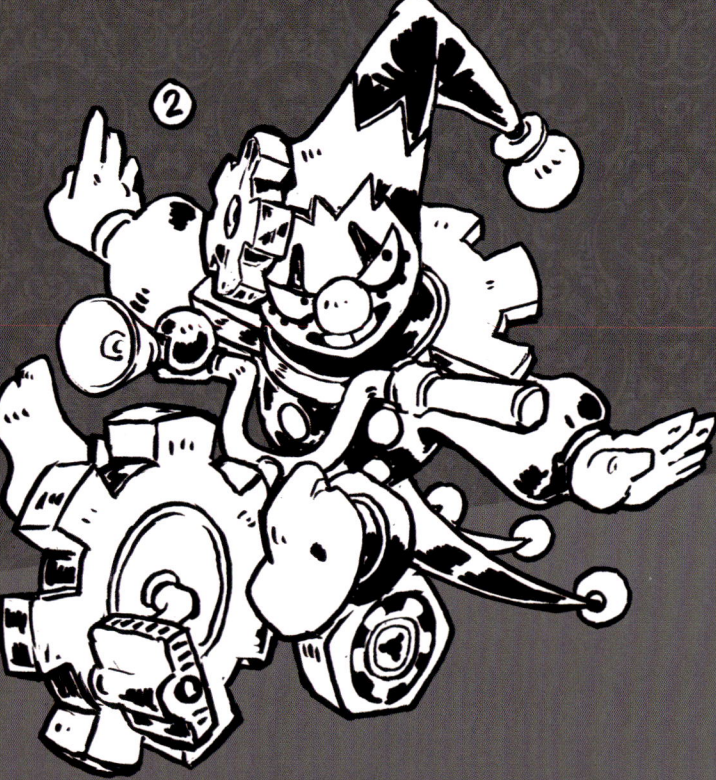

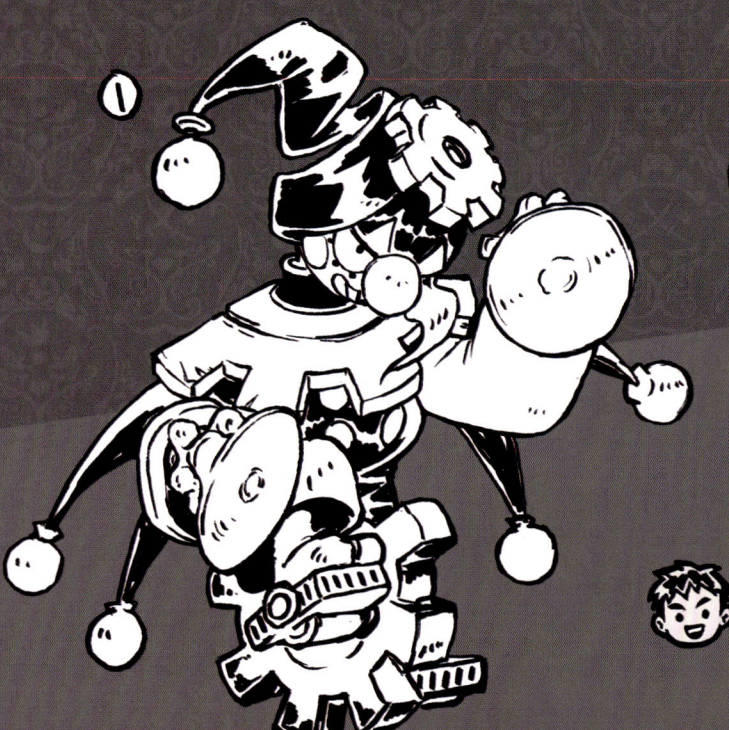

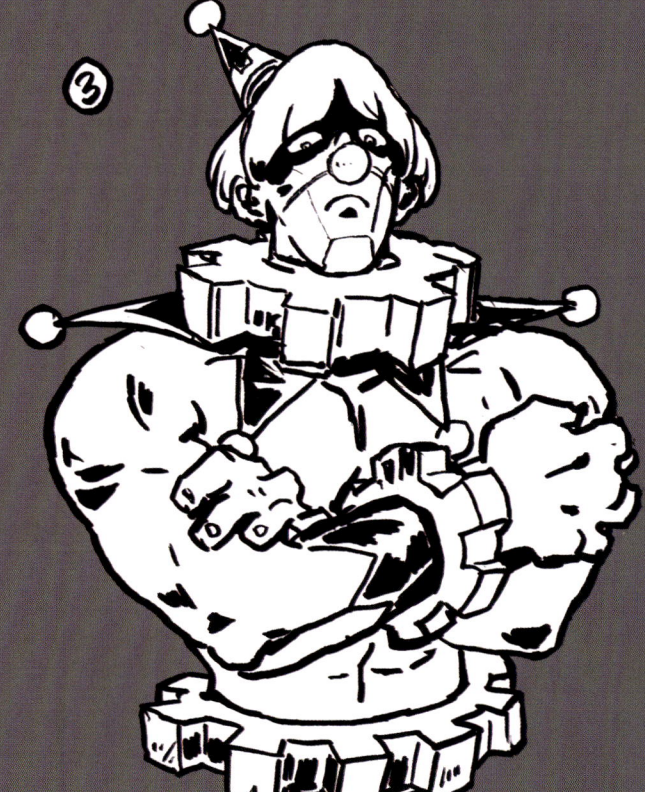

BRYCE: **#1** and **#2** – As close as possible to the prompt as I could figure out – aka, the references you attached + a clockwork element and my own expansion of what might be fun. There's a couple built-in ideas here. First, notice the cogs on their heads. I think they could do a *Dragon Ball*-style dance sequence where they literally combine at the head, transforming into their boss form. This implies that the combination is less of the conventional mech that you had in the brief, but it might be too fun to pass up. It can also still be a mech as you described, but I'll leave that to your discretion.

One of the playful ways I imagine these characters moving around is on their cog-wheeled vehicles: a cog unicycle and cog big-wheeler. I imagine them riding up the walls and triggering switches that alter the rooms. For example, when you first enter, they talk to you, taunting you with silly dialogue, and then run away by riding up the walls and triggering switches that are now out of your reach.

#3 – A *very* off-the-wall idea. Basically, I was trying to think of a unique approach to the conventional 'silly clown duo' and thought you'd find it funny if one of the twins was just ... not. But, before we meet the second twin, the first one constantly says, 'Wait until you meet my twin brother, hee-hee!' It could also be used for a one-off joke; one interaction where Pouf attempts to trick you into thinking that he's looked like that the whole time, or something similar.

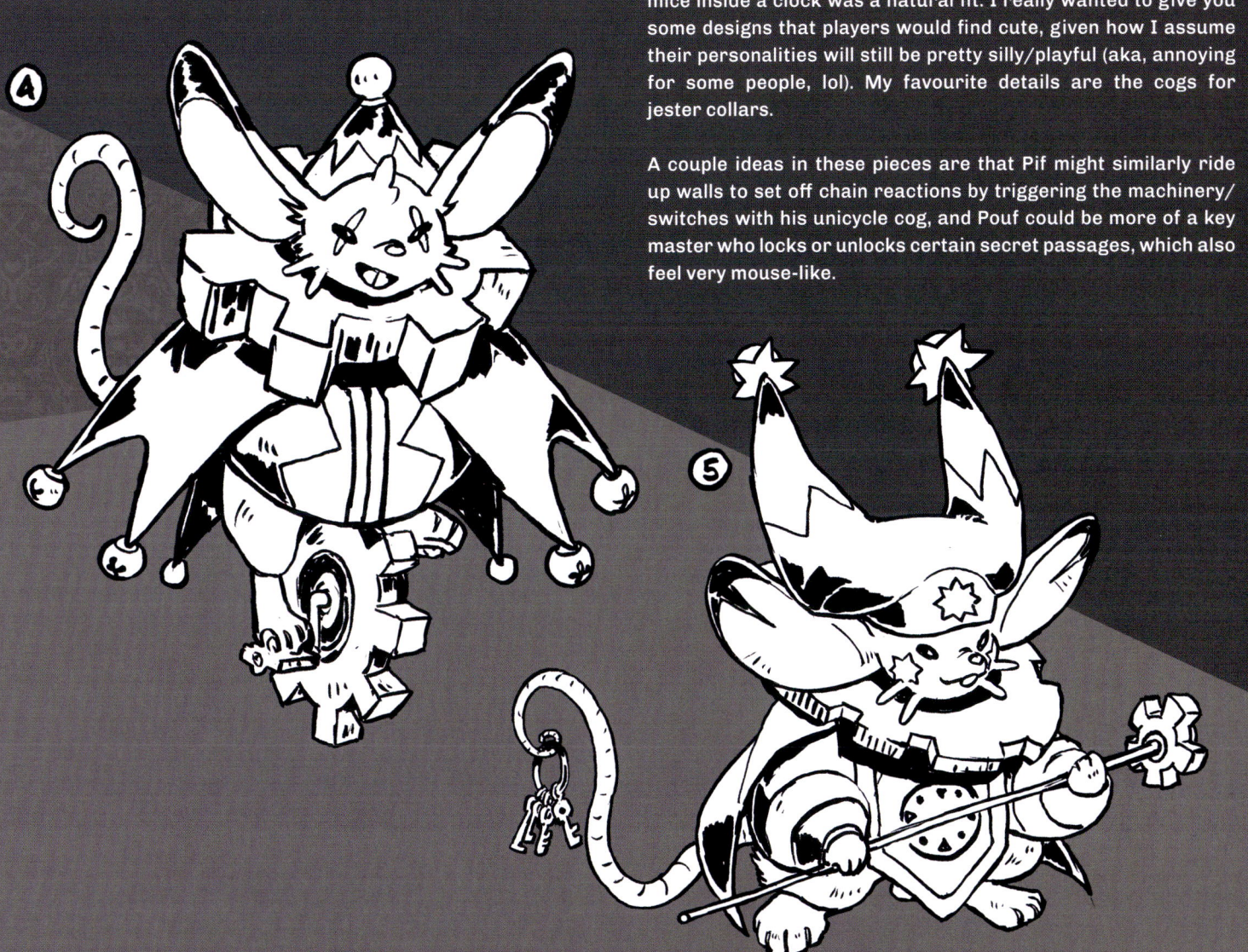

#4 and **#5** – Similarly, I wanted to give you a very different approach from Zorn and Thorn's clown look and thought that mice inside a clock was a natural fit. I really wanted to give you some designs that players would find cute, given how I assume their personalities will still be pretty silly/playful (aka, annoying for some people, lol). My favourite details are the cogs for jester collars.

A couple ideas in these pieces are that Pif might similarly ride up walls to set off chain reactions by triggering the machinery/switches with his unicycle cog, and Pouf could be more of a key master who locks or unlocks certain secret passages, which also feel very mouse-like.

THIERRY: It took a lot of mulling over, but I went with #1 and #2 since they will be the first two characters we meet inside the clock and 'lift the veil' on the DLC's theme. To that effect, I think everything is better served with more on-the-nose designs. So, despite really liking all options, I think it's best to properly set the tone rather than start off with a twist within the reveal, which is already a surprise. I think #1 and #2 will help ground the change in theme and make sure there isn't confusion that we're in evil-circus mode.

I absolutely love the *Dragon Ball* dance idea with the connecting cogs, but we do need Pantouf to be a separate entity that they can fight alongside and later enter. I also like the idea of their cog wheels activating stuff, so this got me thinking they could summon Pantouf by locking in their head gears and driving in perfect circles; their wheels can spin a giant cog in the ground that allows Pantouf to emerge.

Let me know how you feel about that. I think that could be a cool way to keep Pantouf separate while still giving them the Potara earrings moment!

I think we should totally keep option #3 as a clockwork Boulder Douche of sorts, or maybe even Pantouf himself, imagining him bigger and something we could fight Meduso-style where damage shows. Eventually, as we remove the skin layer, only the frame is left and Artificer can use it as a base for the Arcane Golem. Just an idea, though – I'm sure you already have a Pantouf in mind (though the tearing-off-the-skin idea might still be cool regardless of its design).

Option #4 and #5 are too cute to pass up. IMO, we should turn them into regular enemies, maybe just by replacing the cog unicycle on #4 with a circus ball. It's just a proposition; if there are things you absolutely want to do instead, that's fine. I'm just in love with everything on this sheet, lol.

Pif

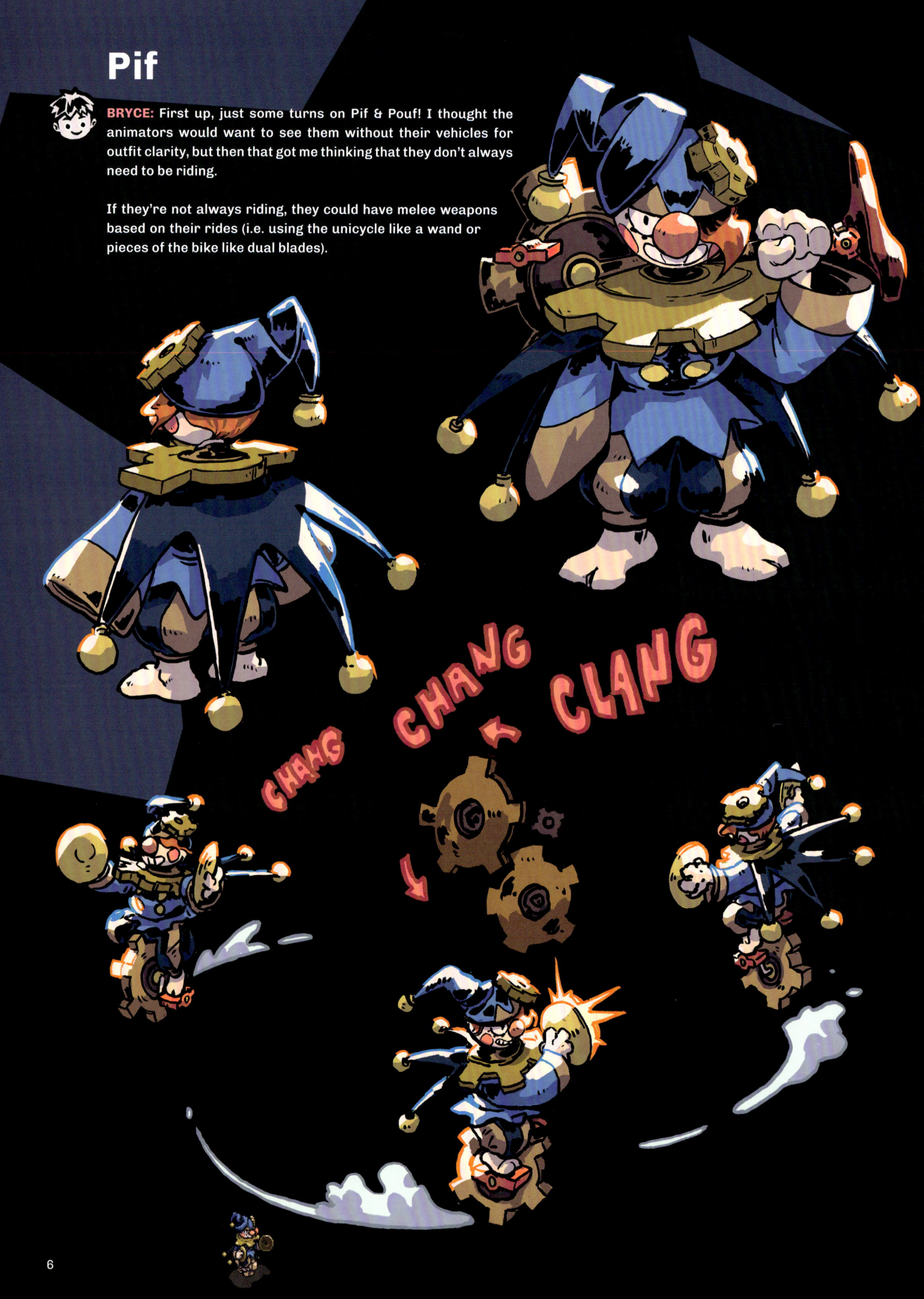

BRYCE: First up, just some turns on Pif & Pouf! I thought the animators would want to see them without their vehicles for outfit clarity, but then that got me thinking that they don't always need to be riding.

If they're not always riding, they could have melee weapons based on their rides (i.e. using the unicycle like a wand or pieces of the bike like dual blades).

CHANG CHANG CLANG

BRYCE: The melee attack has a wide 'up' animation where the unicycle spins really fast before he swings it like a two-handed blade.

 THIERRY: Yes to all of this! Using the vehicles as weapons is also going to allow for cool assembling and disassembling transitions that will bank on the toy/clockwork side of things. Maybe the head gears locking and them driving could also be cool as a tornado-type, ultimate-combo attack so we can see the weapons becoming vehicles in combat as well.

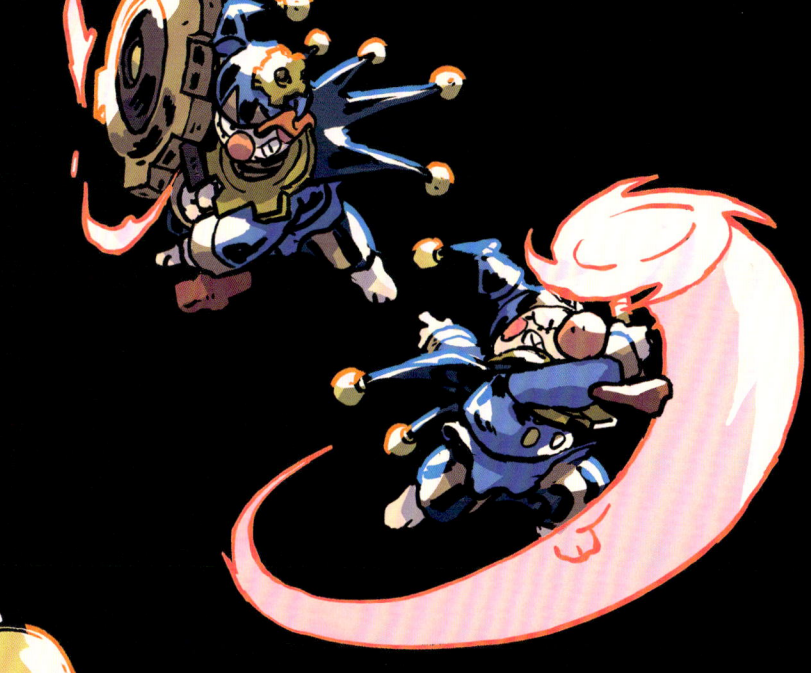

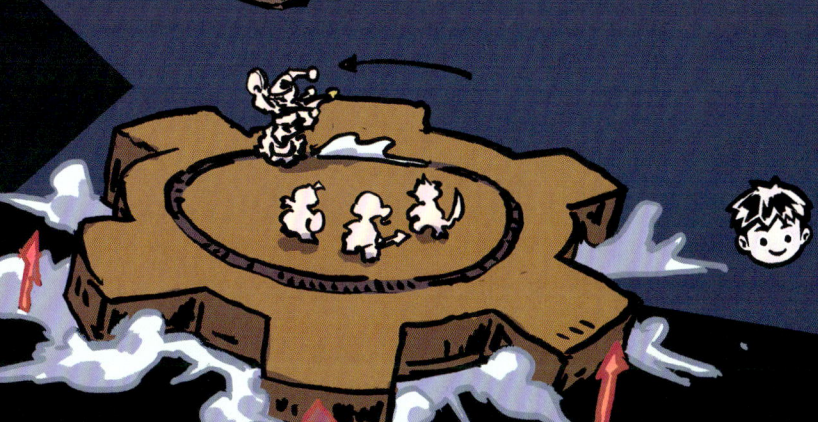

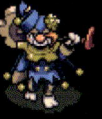 **BRYCE:** I'm thinking that his basic unicycle circle ride can be used for three potential actions: a debuff to the player, buff to Pouf, or lastly, used to turn a giant cog that the battle is taking place on, which could cause a variety of chain reactions such as environmental attacks (like objects falling or triggering a giant hammer to hit the player). Simultaneously, it could also cause the giant cog to rise and reveal the mecha.

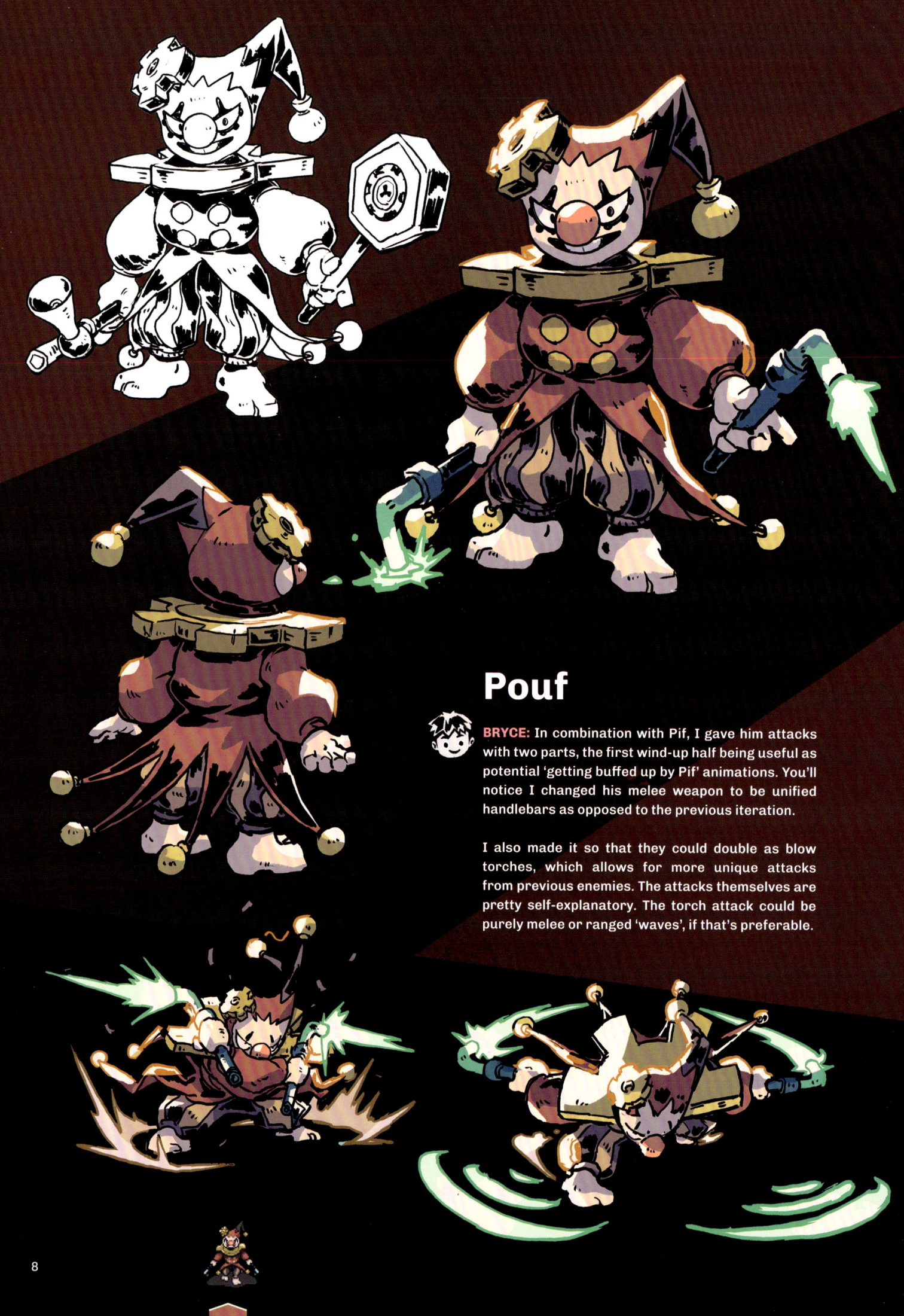

Pouf

BRYCE: In combination with Pif, I gave him attacks with two parts, the first wind-up half being useful as potential 'getting buffed up by Pif' animations. You'll notice I changed his melee weapon to be unified handlebars as opposed to the previous iteration.

I also made it so that they could double as blow torches, which allows for more unique attacks from previous enemies. The attacks themselves are pretty self-explanatory. The torch attack could be purely melee or ranged 'waves', if that's preferable.

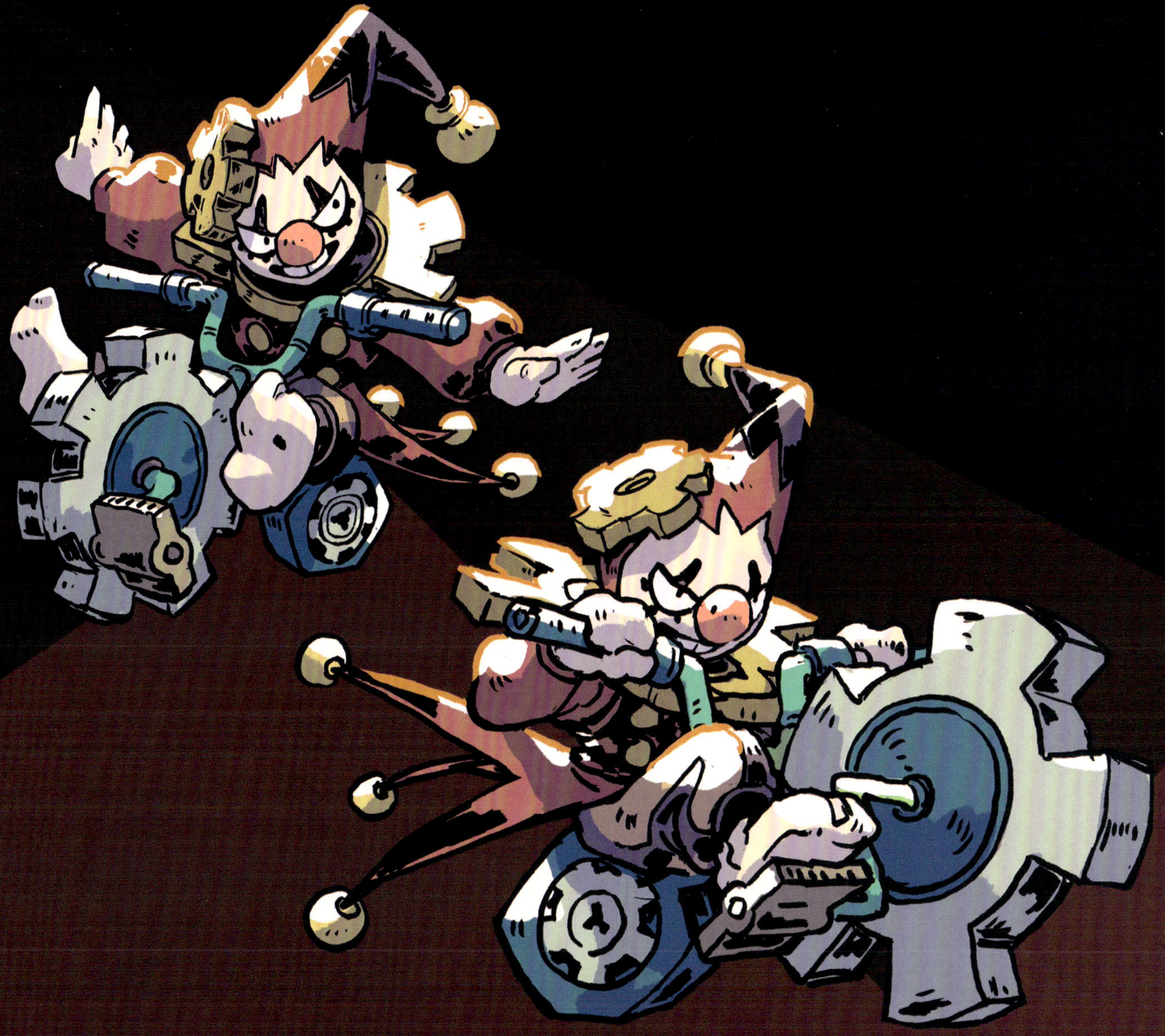

BRYCE: I've gone for very playful primary colours (but slightly desaturated to not be too wacky) to lean into the clockwork and clown theme, but let me know if you want me to try something else.

My gut tells me that the backgrounds would be duller/browns to look like clockwork pieces, which would help with making the characters pop out.

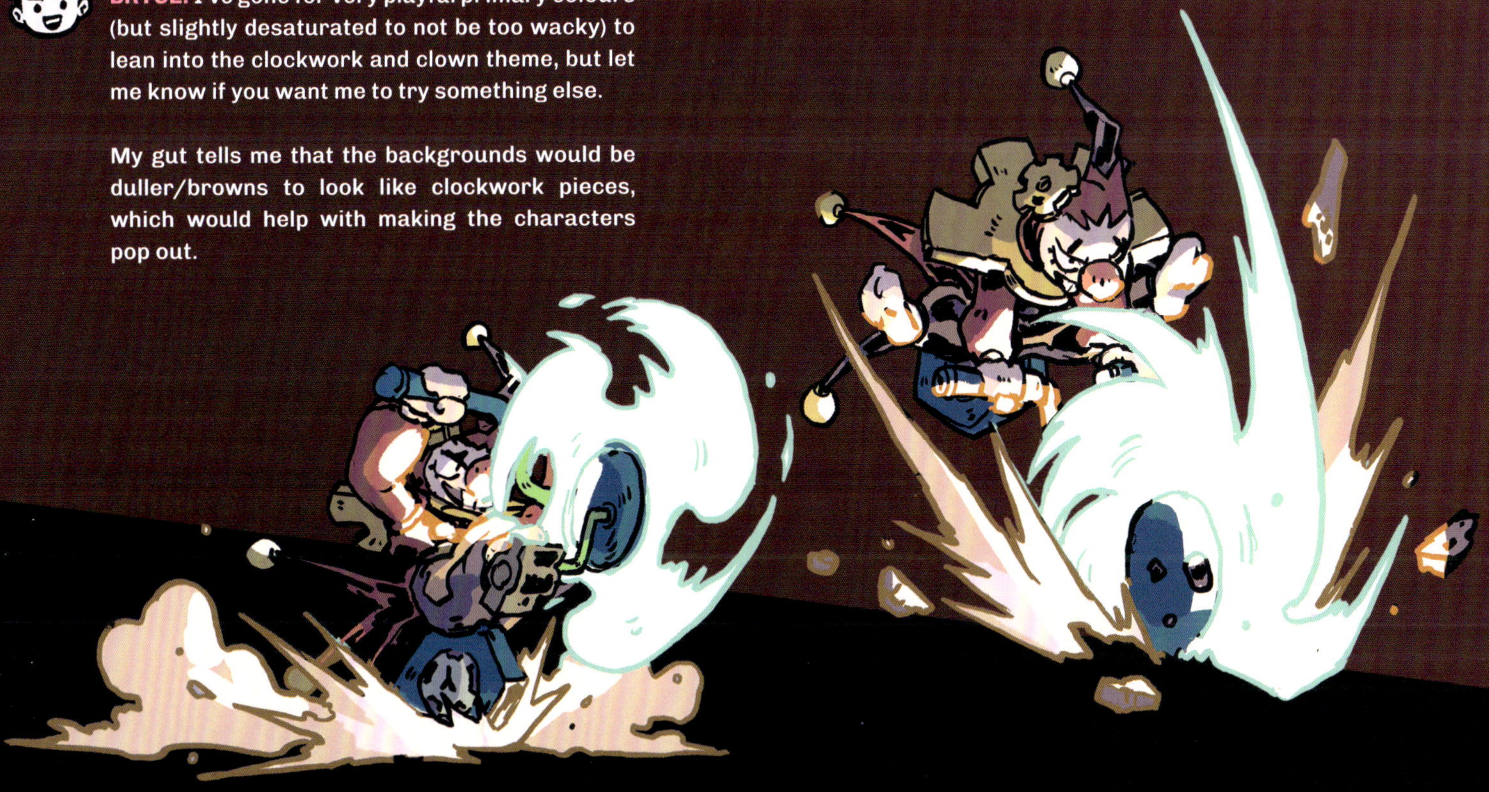

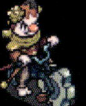

Fardush the Train Conductor

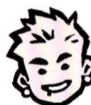

THIERRY: As clockwork as all the others, though this one is a lifesize toy-train driver, so he's maybe less on the circus/fair side? I feel like you probably already see this guy in your mind so I'll stop here, but referencess are available if needed.

BRYCE: Some options for our conductor, Fardush! I really wanted to use Fardush as an opportunity to play with what it means to be a clockwork-based life form, and hope that this range of designs will help us figure out what to do with the villagers as well as some of the enemies.

#1 – First impression for what a clockwork-based life form might be like. It's basically something akin to an action figure.

#2 – A more basic humanoid look but with random clockwork pieces distinguishing them as different. I felt like part of your brief hints that Narcissist Zale and Wolf Valere have followers that still need to look cool and be clockwork (which might be a tall order, tbh), so I carved out this option to allow for both. Notice the Iron Man chest piece, which is also a clock.

#3 – We could make the clockwork folks even more ephemeral and different in proportion from the other more recent villagers, maybe more like the molekin in height. The idea is that they always have huge wind-up knobs on their backs and big, black, mage-esque eyes. This particular Fardush concept is a silly nod to Mario's design, but in colour. We could make that reference more subtle or obvious if you're into it.

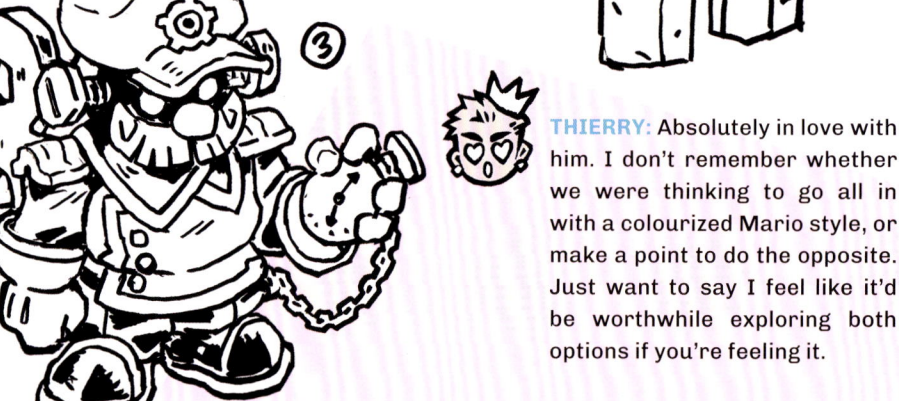

THIERRY: Absolutely in love with him. I don't remember whether we were thinking to go all in with a colourized Mario style, or make a point to do the opposite. Just want to say I feel like it'd be worthwhile exploring both options if you're feeling it.

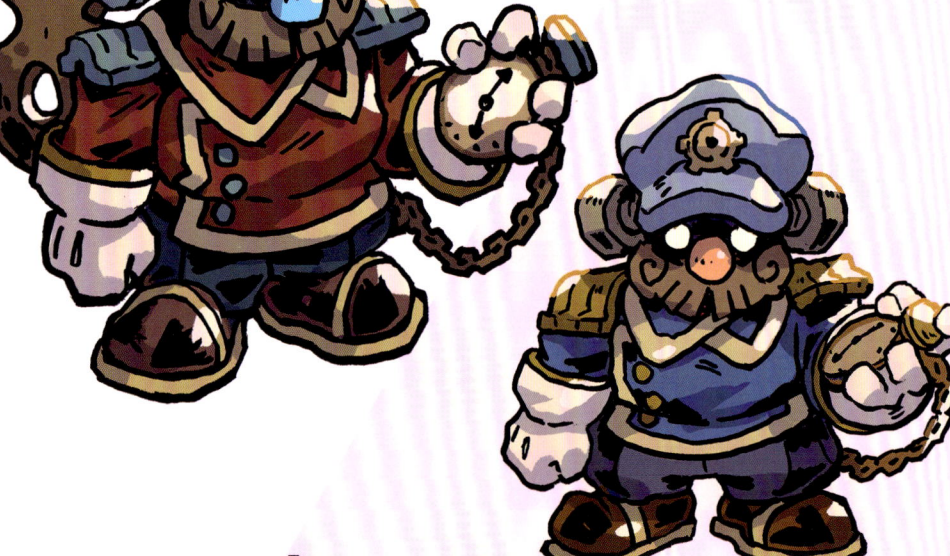

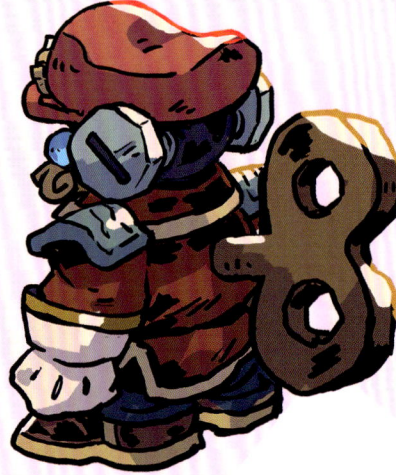

Horloge Villagers

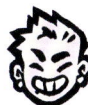

THIERRY: Here, we just need a good old villagers sheet. Each of the clockwork life forms must emphasize the whole circus/fair thing. I kind of just want to see what you'll do with the prompt, so I'm not including any references, but feel free to ask if you'd rather see them! If all else fails, just think 'wacky clockwork circus fair', lol. My only specific request here would be to make sure one is a bully/bouncer/strongman body type to be able to double as the prison guard that Valtraid punches.

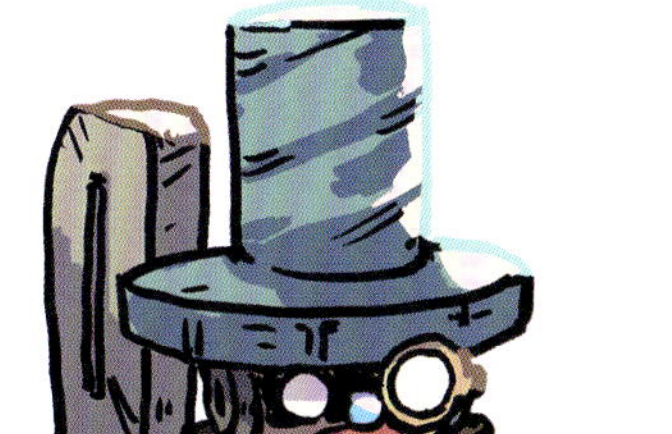

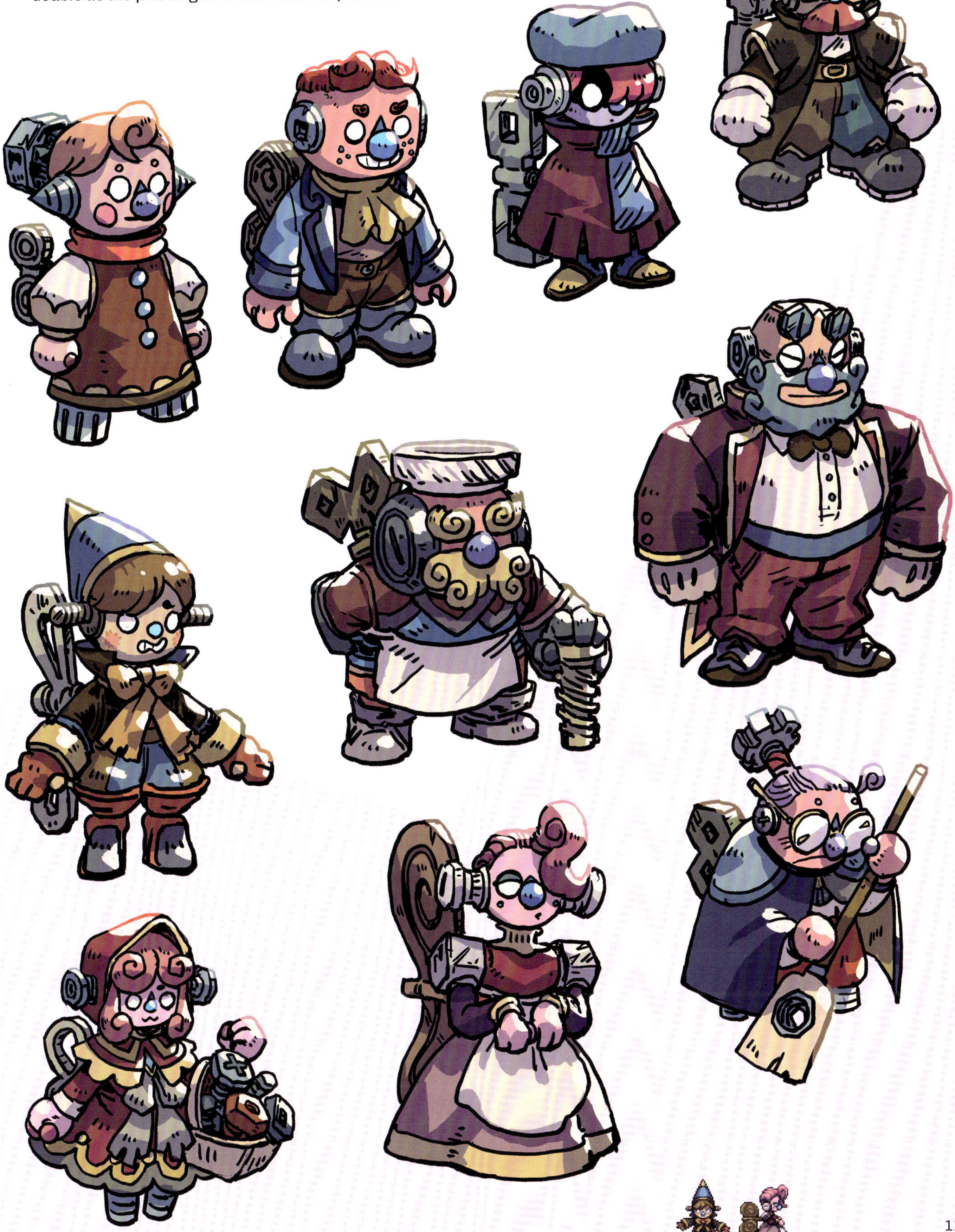

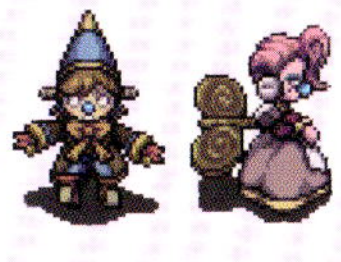

Crazy Train Boss

THIERRY: This is the angry boss train we will fight to tame and bring back on the rails for Fardush to drive us around. It should be a normal-sized train when compared to our character sprites, but I feel like a toy-train design would be really cool. Any ideas for special moves/attacks are welcome, too!

BRYCE: Soot-Sprite Powered – Pollution-and-smoke-themed train that doesn't have to move like a train at all, but as more of a gaseous monster. My favourite bit is that one of the soot sprites can blow a loud train choo-choo whistle and cause it to let out clouds of smoke. I like the ability to use smoke as limbs since it'll make the attacks easier (?) to animate, or at least give them more variety.

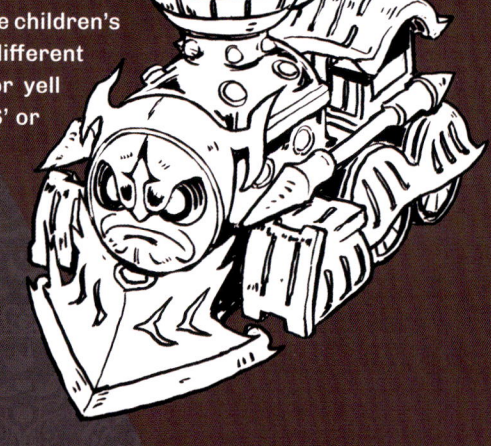

Thanatos the Hell-Engine – An obvious play on *Thomas the Tank Engine* but like, mean, lol. I wanted to give you something more recognizable as a train shape and so this design relies less on a novel design than its playful, dark contrast against the children's character. Attack-wise, it's also harder to imagine its main movement different to a battering ram, but the mouth of the angry face could also shoot or yell things. All caps dialogue like, 'ALL PASSENGERS MUST CLEAR THE TRACKS' or 'UNTICKETED PASSENGERS ARE SUBJECT TO PENALTIES.'

Gentleman's Train – Notice the moustache and monocle design on the face of the train. A much more clock-heavy design where the personality of the train is a bit more fancy, gilded, and Nouveau Gothic. I still imagine nonsensical train dialogue like the previous design but with less-intense diction. Instead, the speech is more playful, polite, and gentlemanly.

Also, notice that the rail that's normally just there to connect the wheels has been transformed into something like a blade scythe. I also think the giant cog chimney on the back can be used to spew out projectiles like steam or coal.

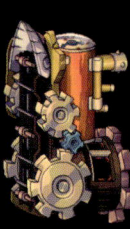

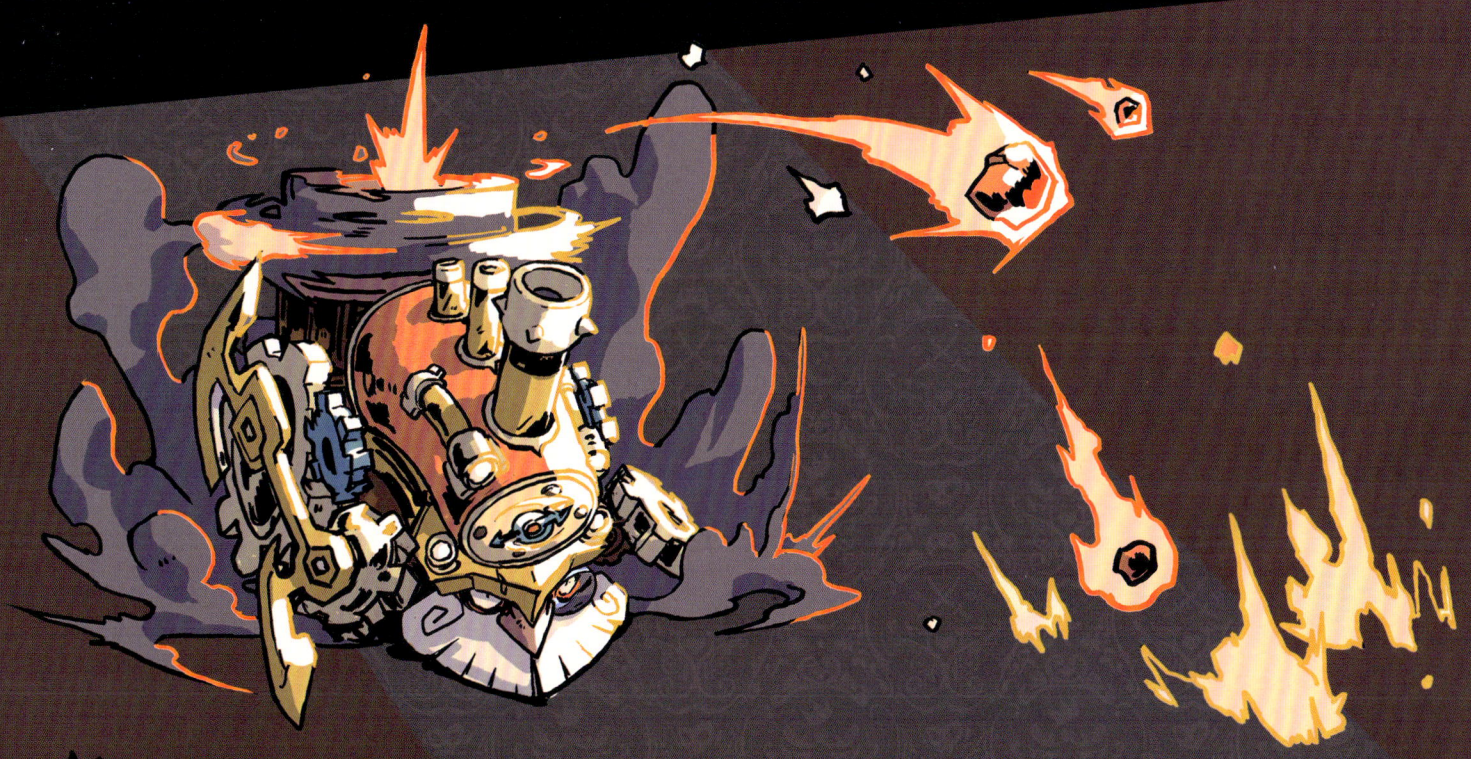

THIERRY: The more I pictured it, the more I kept thinking we just need a 'basics done right' train, and #3 is just that: it's something we won't need to talk to and really captures the vibe of chasing after a wild, elusive animal in need of taming. In doing the *FF6* homage fight, he will also be better with less 'personality', just blurting out special attacks like 'Boarding Pass' before ramming into a character that's forced to waste two turns being a passenger or something.

Oh, and one more thing about train #3 is that it feels visually 'deconstructable and reconstructable'. We could kind of break it down by beating it and have to find the side blades and chimney again by doing the other dungeons!

BRYCE: Admittedly, it's hard to make actions for this guy because of how structural he is. I originally sketched out a crazy melee attack, but felt like if it was annoying for me to draw the keyframes, then animating it would probably be insane. So, to explain the attacks, the one above is revving up the engine (a big choo-choo SFX seems in order here). I put in some coal projectiles, but in retrospect this might feel too similar to the volcano toad. So, an alternative idea would be steaming up the whole battlefield so all attacks miss while it's in effect? Or just AOE. Below is a large blade attack where he first disconnects the rail on the wheels, cocks it back so that it turns into a hook/scythe, and then does a huge jumping spin attack.

CLICK

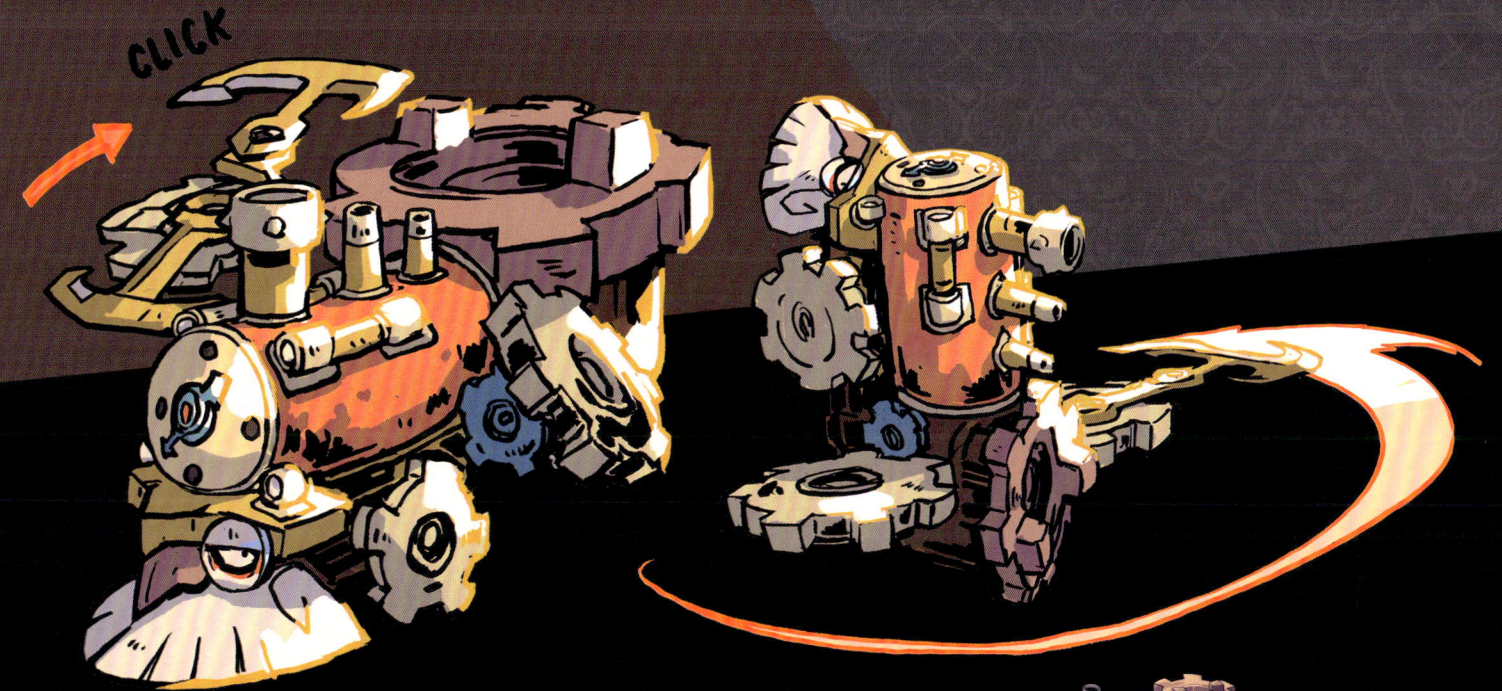

Clockwork Jungle Enemies

 THIERRY: This dungeon is a shorter one, so we only need two enemies for it. Clockwork jungle creatures could be cool, and/or something more to do with the rail/train aspect of things, like a mechanic of sorts.

 BRYCE: Cargo Lizard – A companion enemy for the big train. He's not as 'cool', but perhaps the thematic trappings are worthwhile enough. Gameplay-wise, my idea is that his cargo behaves like shields, meaning he takes no damage until they're all destroyed first.

Gear-Butt Babboon – FYI, all of the following enemies are inspired by my trip to the Singapore Zoo. Basically, the real-life baboon's giant red butt is insane and that's all I wanted to focus on here, using big red gears to emulate it. It could be a flourish thing, but we could also motivate some unique attacks with it (rotating the gears to wind up a 'projectile', lol). If that's too juvenile, he can also just do a big tail swing for us to see the big gears in action.

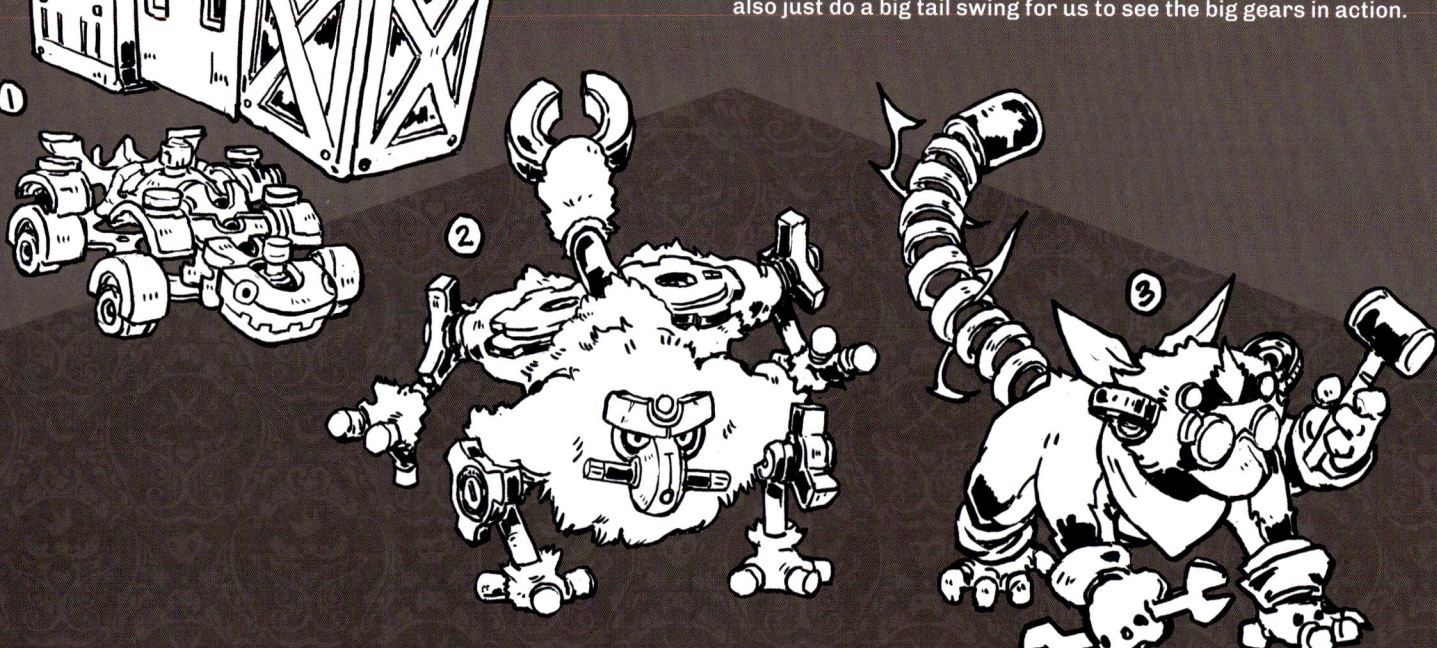

Lemur Coiler – Whereas baboon's have impressive butts, lemur tails are relatively huge and long. So, a lemur with a thick electric coil for a tail makes sense. The other tools are really just for flavour, tbh. But if you need a healer type, this could be a cute and novel enemy to serve that dual function.

Sundial Lizard – Not really an actual sundial, of course. I just wanted to make the shapes of the clock face resemble the jungle lizards that have huge neck frills. Functionally, I imagine he has to do spinning or springing movements. I like to imagine his passive animation is just his head rotating like the hands of the clock in that signature sharp and twitchy sort of way.

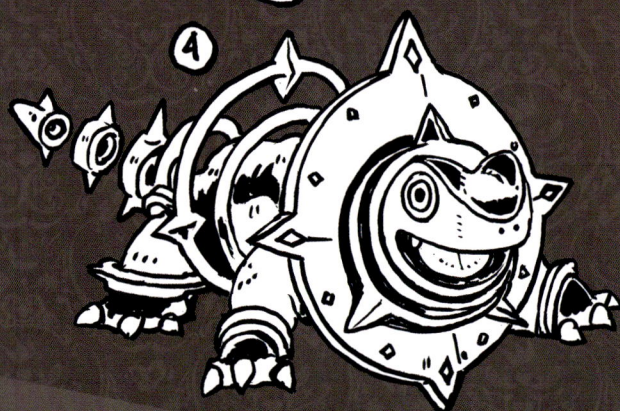

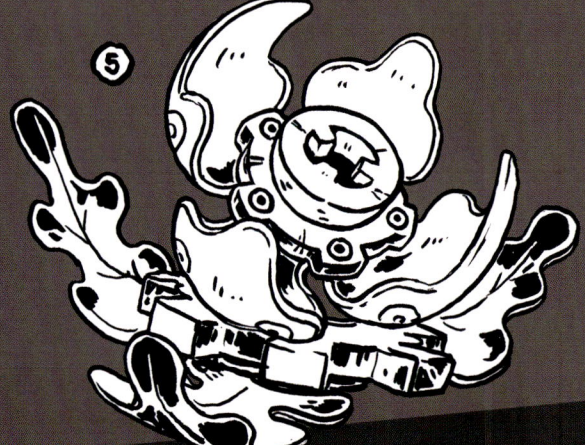

Gear Flower – In case you didn't notice, I really put a lot of thought into making unique enemies that would also match the jungle theme in a new and exciting way. A flower enemy feels like a good repeatable enemy that won't feel spammy if we kill a bunch.

Also, I imagine you could get away with a single direction, animation-wise, which makes it have less scope. Only downside might be that it's less reusable for other areas. I feel like this one is self-explanatory for ideas on attacks, but I will say that I think the organic nature of the leaves will be a nice contrast against the mechanical movements of the flower pieces.

Lizard Train Cargo

 BRYCE: Some pretty functional, straightforward attacks here. A lunge bite that could double as a ramming kamikaze move, and then a second attack where it arches its back to launch its cargo. Most of this enemy's fun is having different cargo on its back. Either two pieces which can hit (obviously) two different targets for medium damage, or a large cargo for higher, single-target damage. It could also have special cargo like a cage filled with another enemy or TNT.

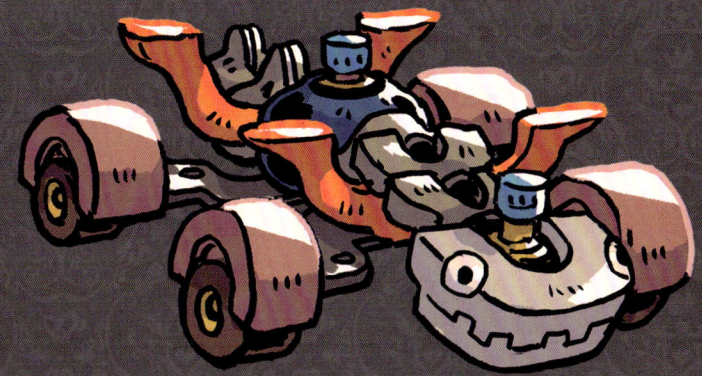

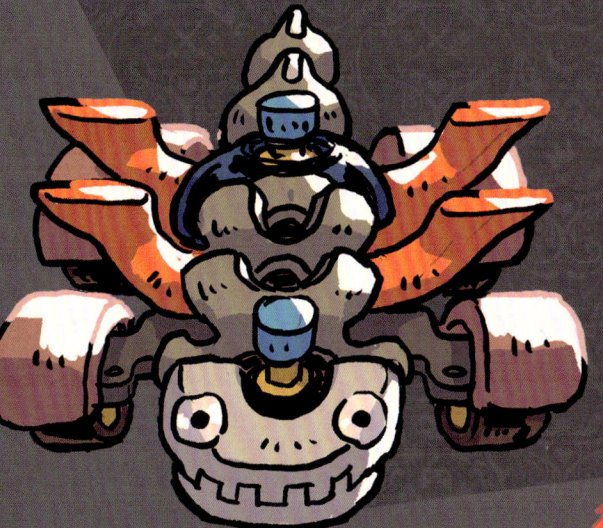

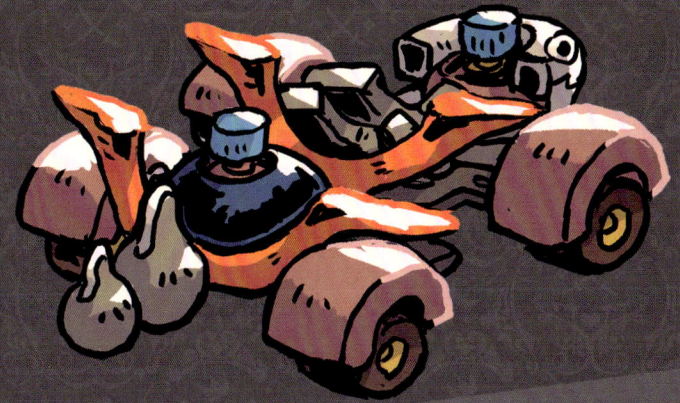

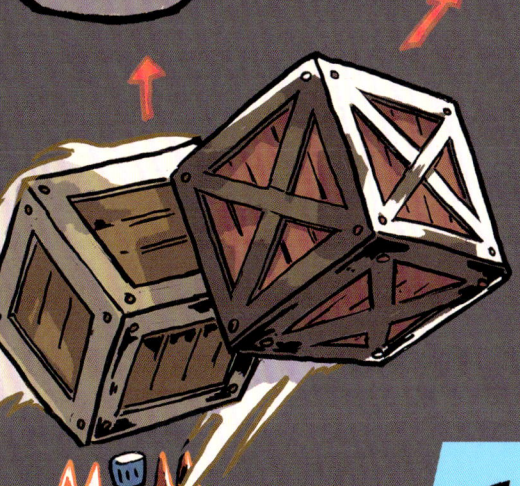

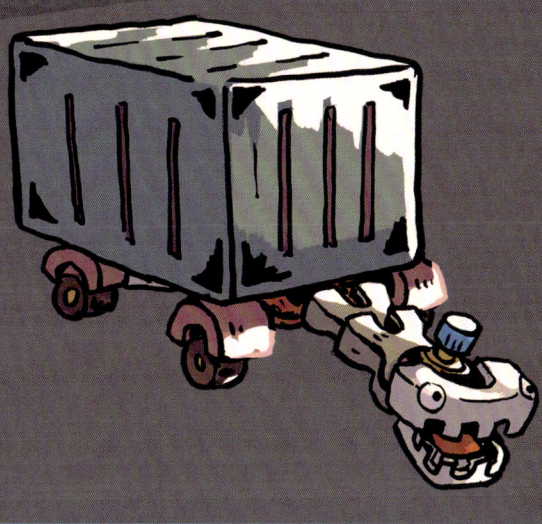

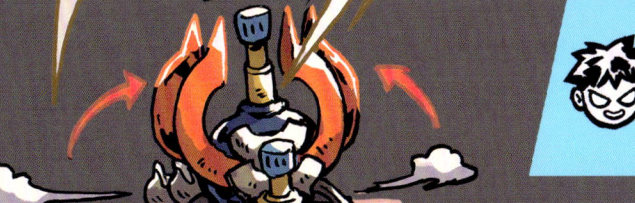

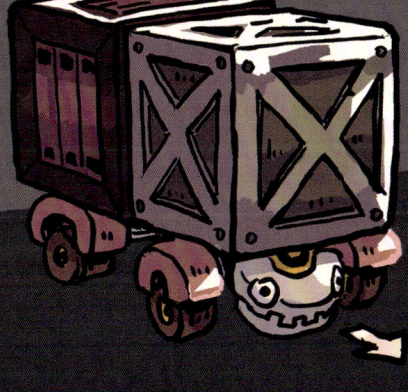 **BRYCE:** My initial thought was that you could target these pieces separately from the lizard itself to break these things – destroying the heavy cargo to avoid taking heavy damage or hitting the TNT with a ranged attack to damage the lizard.

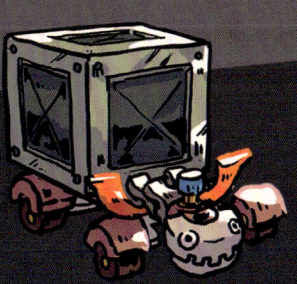

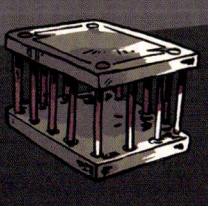

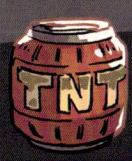

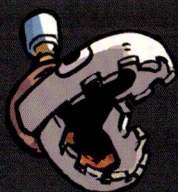

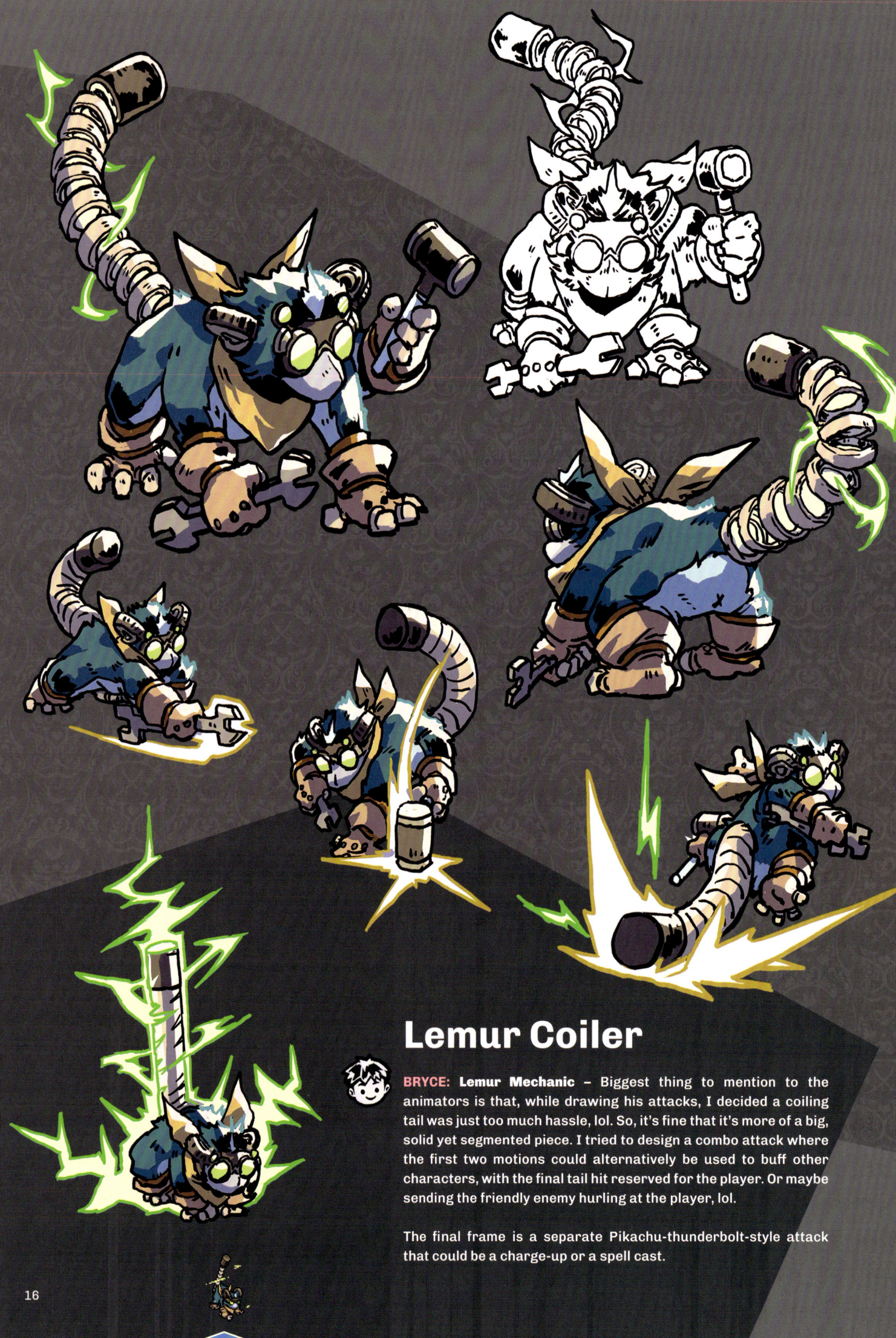

Lemur Coiler

BRYCE: Lemur Mechanic – Biggest thing to mention to the animators is that, while drawing his attacks, I decided a coiling tail was just too much hassle, lol. So, it's fine that it's more of a big, solid yet segmented piece. I tried to design a combo attack where the first two motions could alternatively be used to buff other characters, with the final tail hit reserved for the player. Or maybe sending the friendly enemy hurling at the player, lol.

The final frame is a separate Pikachu-thunderbolt-style attack that could be a charge-up or a spell cast.

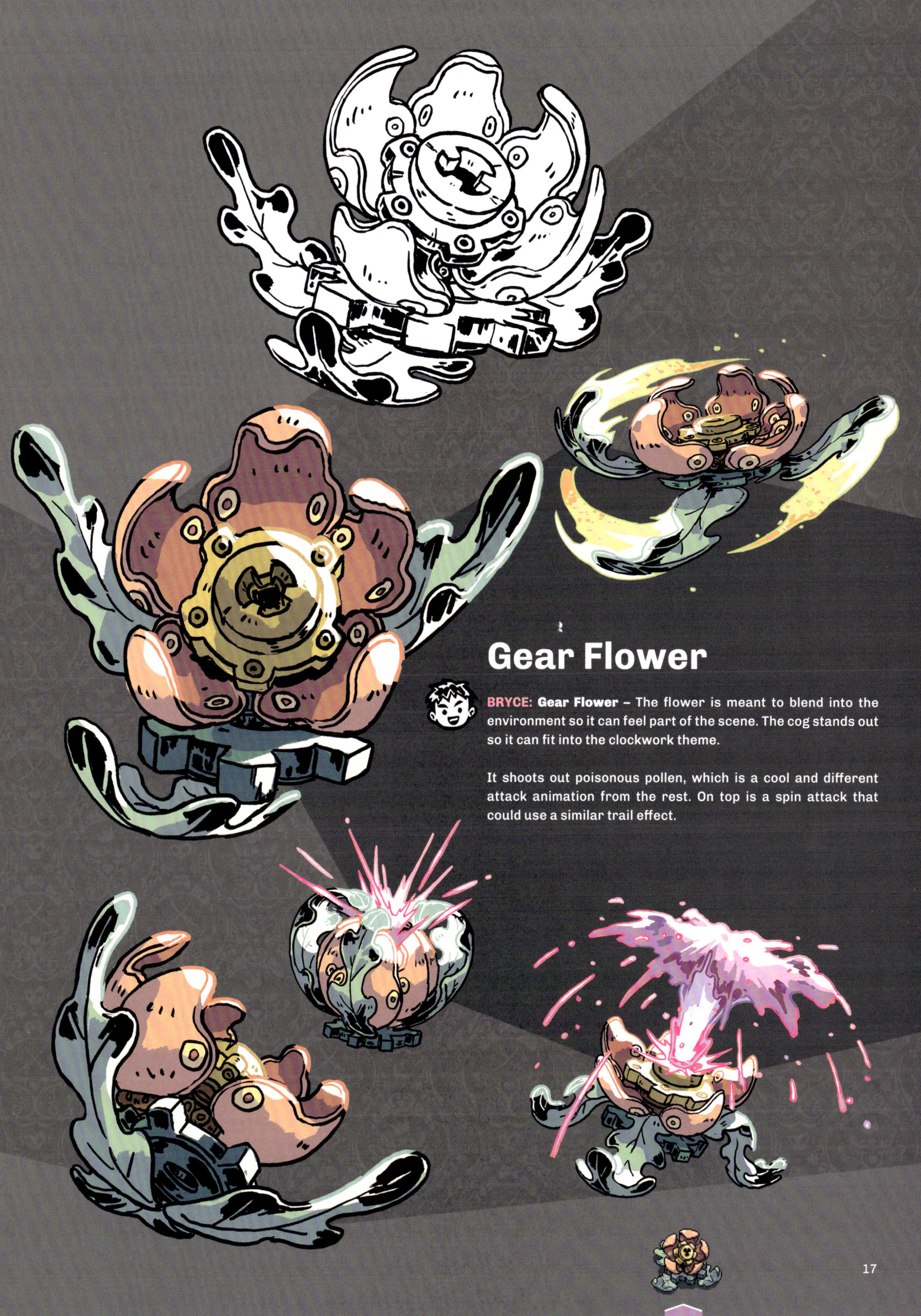

Gear Flower

BRYCE: **Gear Flower** – The flower is meant to blend into the environment so it can feel part of the scene. The cog stands out so it can fit into the clockwork theme.

It shoots out poisonous pollen, which is a cool and different attack animation from the rest. On top is a spin attack that could use a similar trail effect.

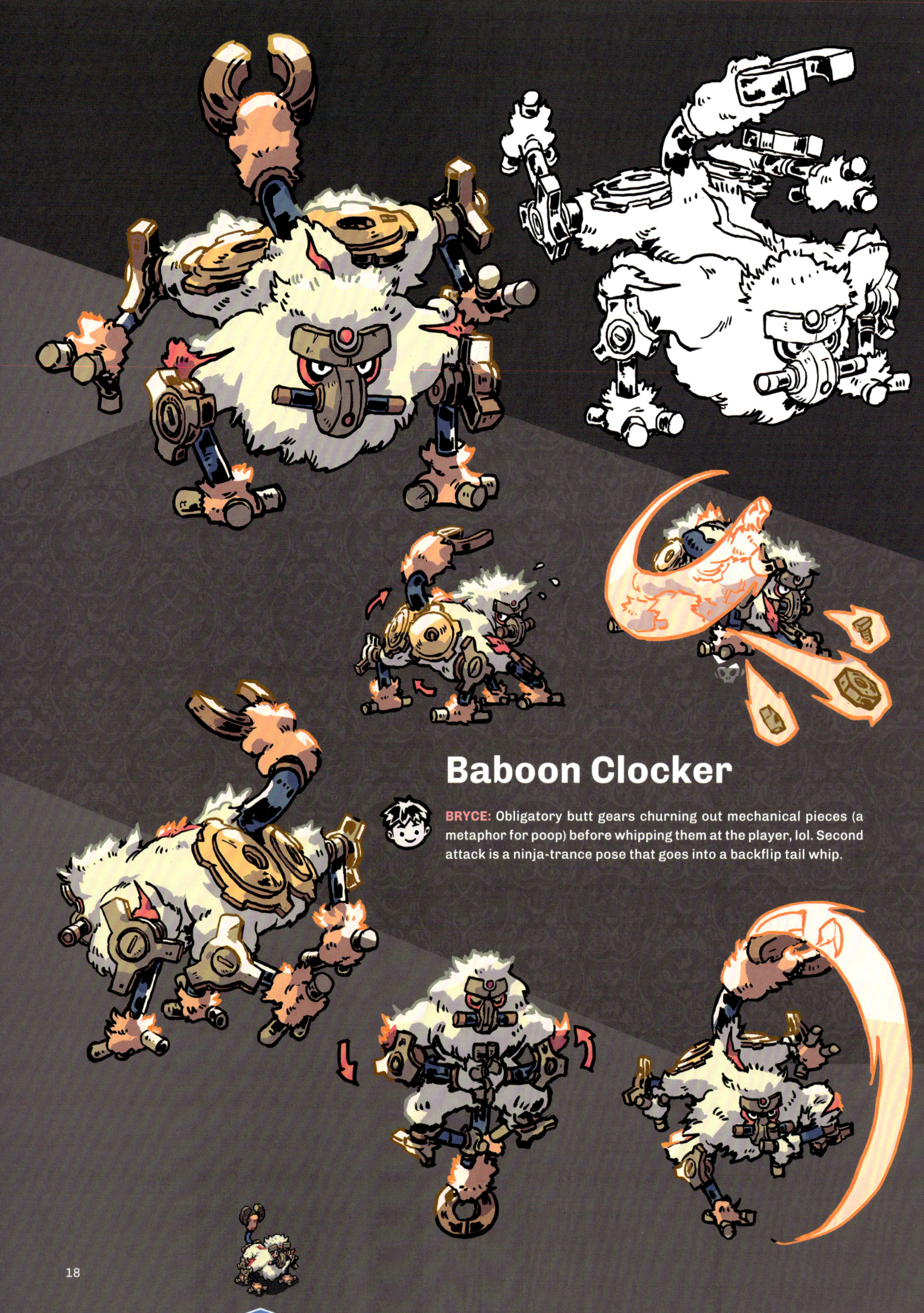

Baboon Clocker

BRYCE: Obligatory butt gears churning out mechanical pieces (a metaphor for poop) before whipping them at the player, lol. Second attack is a ninja-trance pose that goes into a backflip tail whip.

Holy Enemies

THIERRY: We need a good set of 'crazed followers of the light' here. Just thinking of a balanced group including a melee tank, support/caster, and perhaps a ranger or assassin. The angels from *Darksiders* come to mind as a general idea here, but feel free to disregard it if you're feeling anything else. Clockwork, though, with the additional challenge of the silly circus rule, so their attacks should be things like spinning majorette sticks or something.

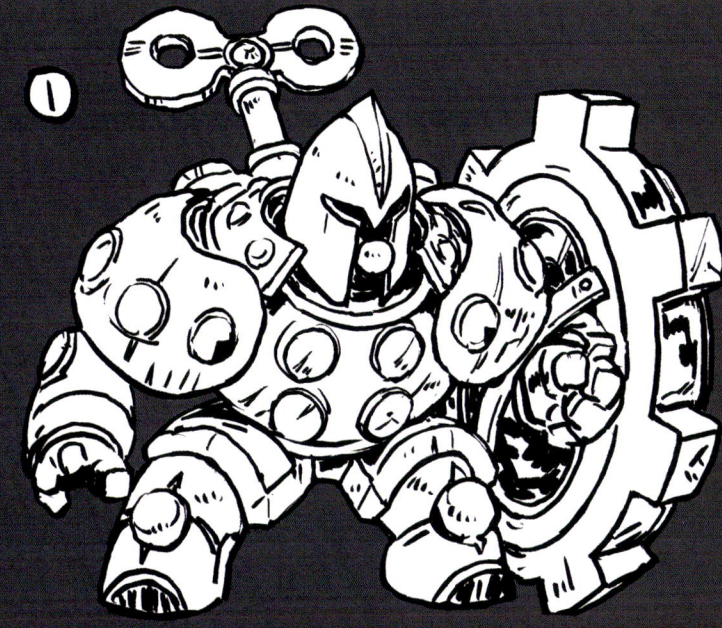

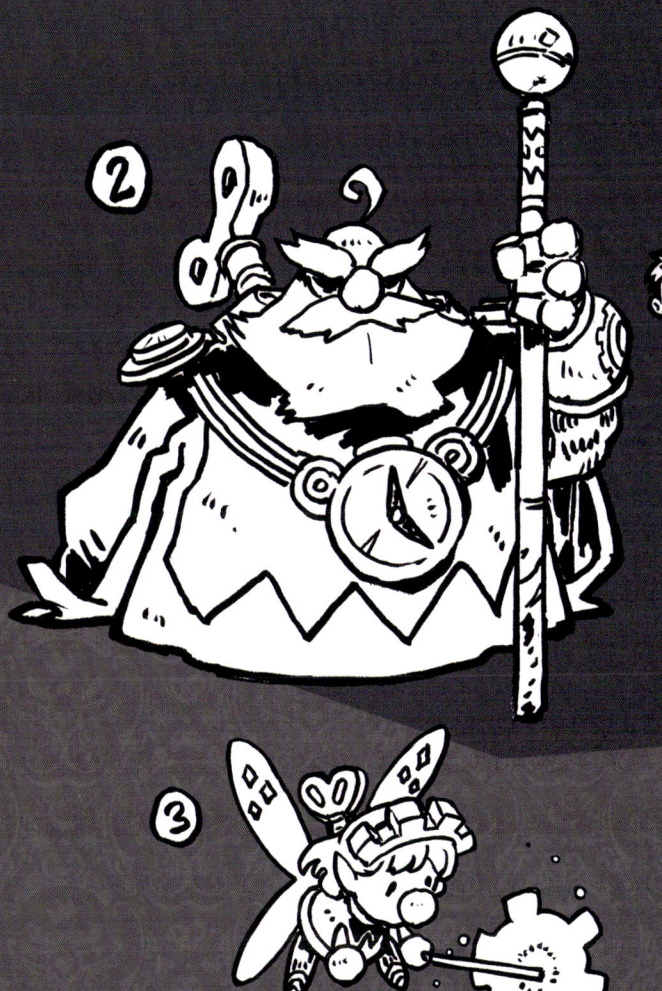

BRYCE: Shield Cog Knight – Notice how he still has the dorky clockwork nose, which is really the unifying element for this group of RPG enemies. I think his attack would be to aggressively roll out the cog, but he holds on to it as it spins, effectively making it like a Sonic the Hedgehog attack. Maybe he can also deflect attack, lol.

Clockwork Wizard – Straightforward wizard, but I really like his dopey body shape. I feel like he basically just bobs up and down when walking without ever showing his feet. The following might be a useful idea for any of these enemies: when he charges up a spell, the crank on his back slowly winds up, and when he releases an attack, it spins super fast.

Cog Navi – I wanted a smaller, animation-friendly enemy that still fits into this RPG theming, so here we have a little fairy mage. The neat thing to point out is that the particle around their wand is a spinning cog – just another way to keep the clockwork theme in there, lol.

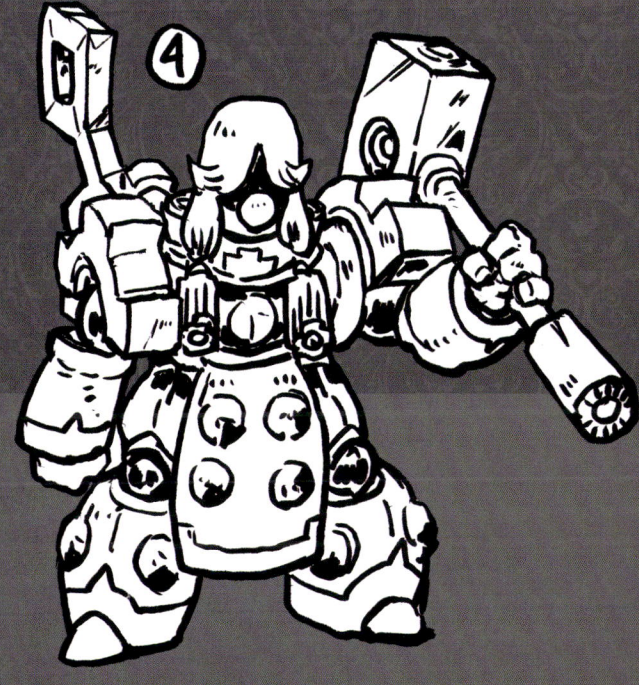

Cog Cleric – A more offensive enemy, but still heavily armoured to match Zale. Similar to #2, maybe it's less about an overt clock reference and more about winding up their back cranks before they attack. For this cleric, it could be something like a charging stance where the cog gets cranked up before releasing into a spinning hammer attack. This character and #3 could also buff the other characters, causing their cranks to spin quickly while receiving the buff.

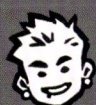

THIERRY: Zale's enemies: I'm bummed we can only make two because they're all really compelling. After throwing it around in my mind, I had to pick Shield Cog Knight and Clockwork Wizard. They'll be a fun pair to fight and complement the ones that bleed from other areas. Super stong silhouettes, too!

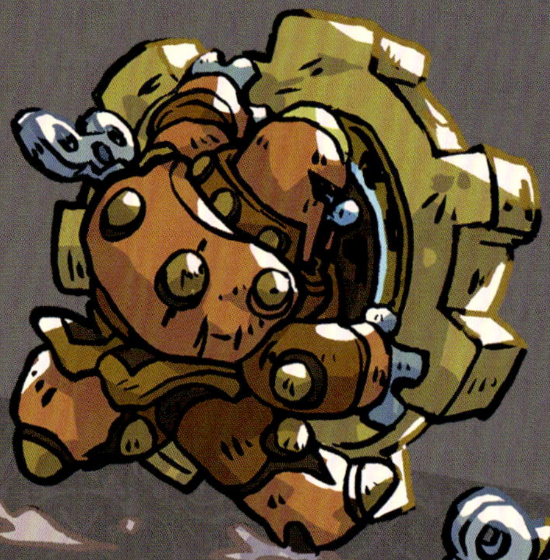

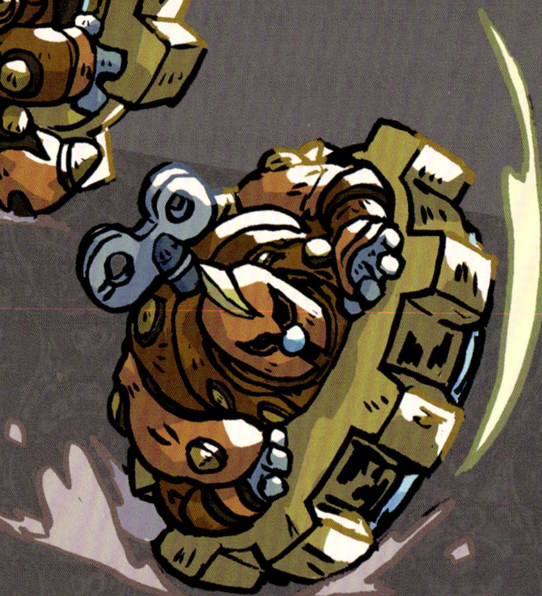

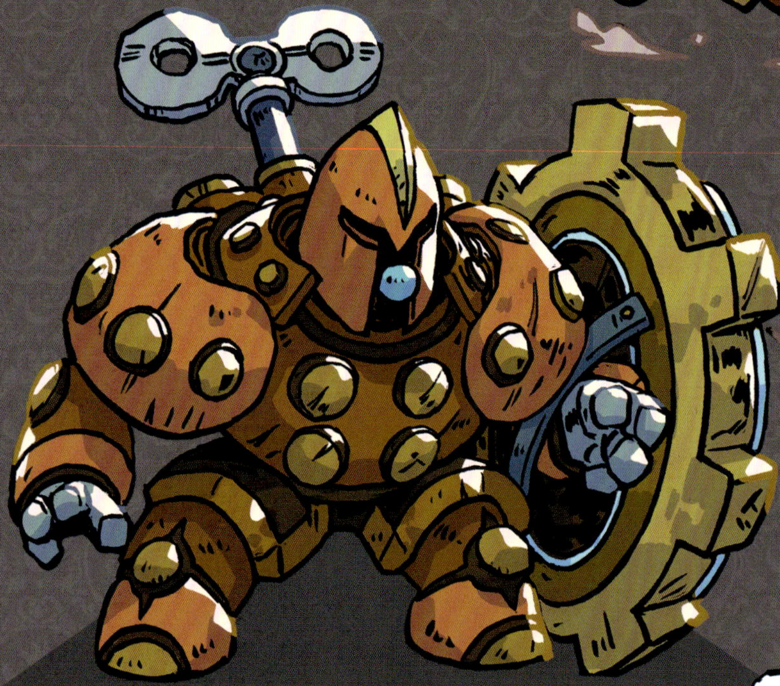

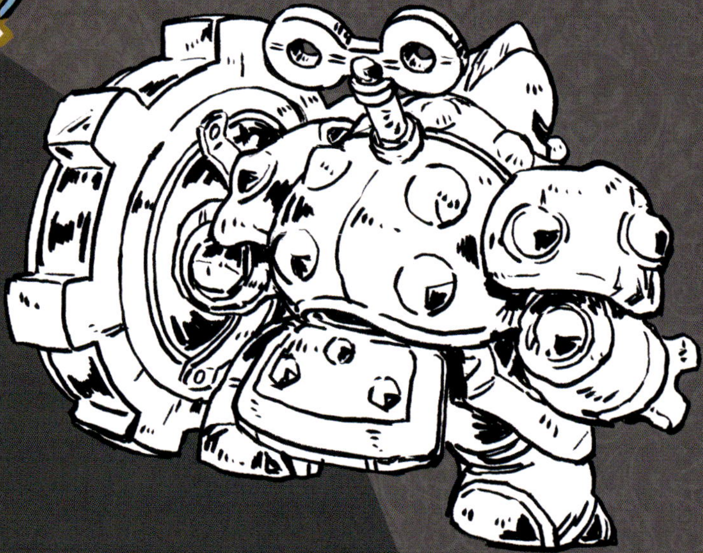

Shield Cog Knight

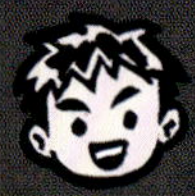

BRYCE: Running start and then rides a cog around, ramming into players.

Generic boomerang toss that can maybe bounce around on player and enemy alike, speeding up enemy attack counters, lol.

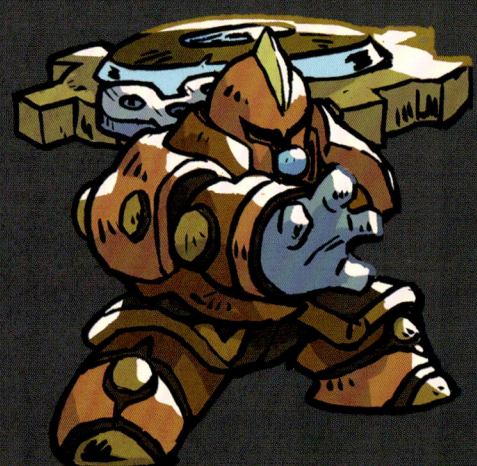

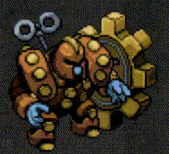

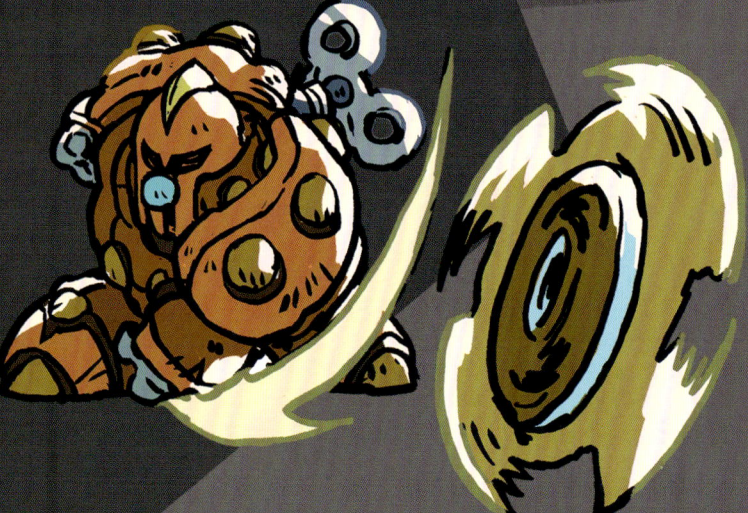

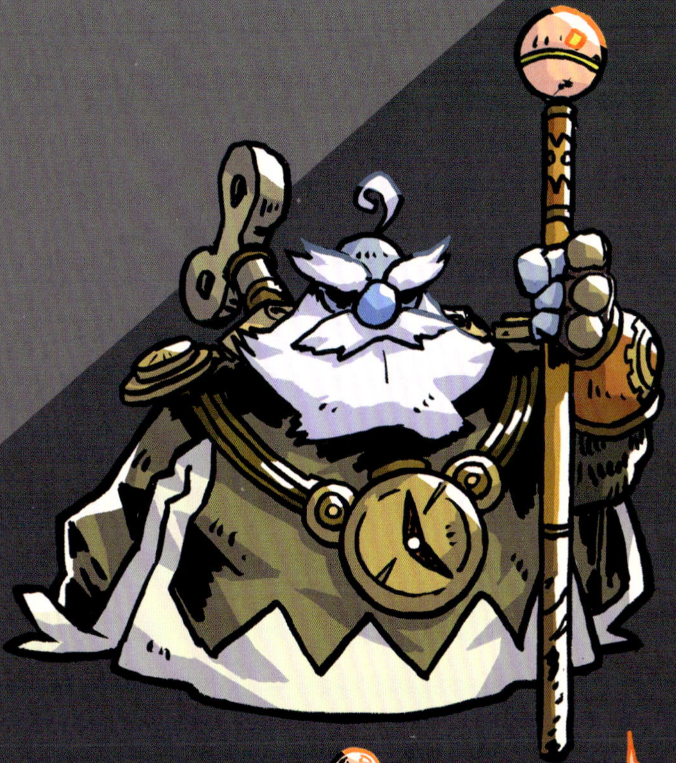

Clockwork Wizard

BRYCE: For the wizard's attacks, two ideas here: it'd be fun and surprising to have such an old guy actually be one of the faster-moving enemies. Like a baton, he unnecessarily twirls his wand to charge up its power before unleashing a volley of non-elemental projectiles that are star/spark themed.

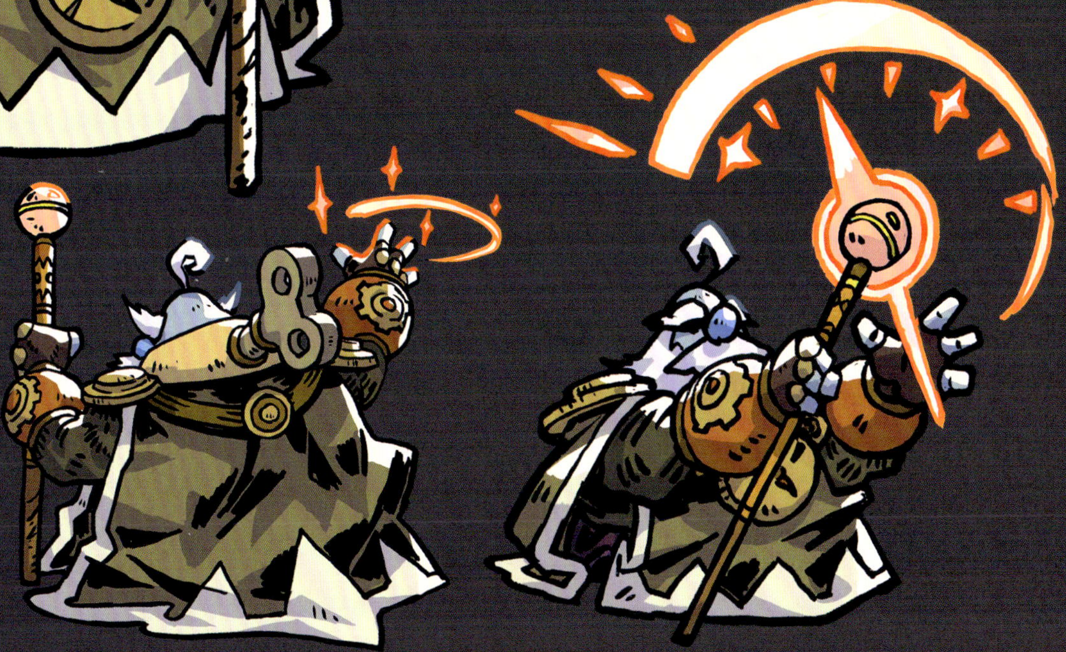

THIERRY: Great ideas, and there's a lot I can tweak in the balancing to support the display of an unexpectedly fast character.

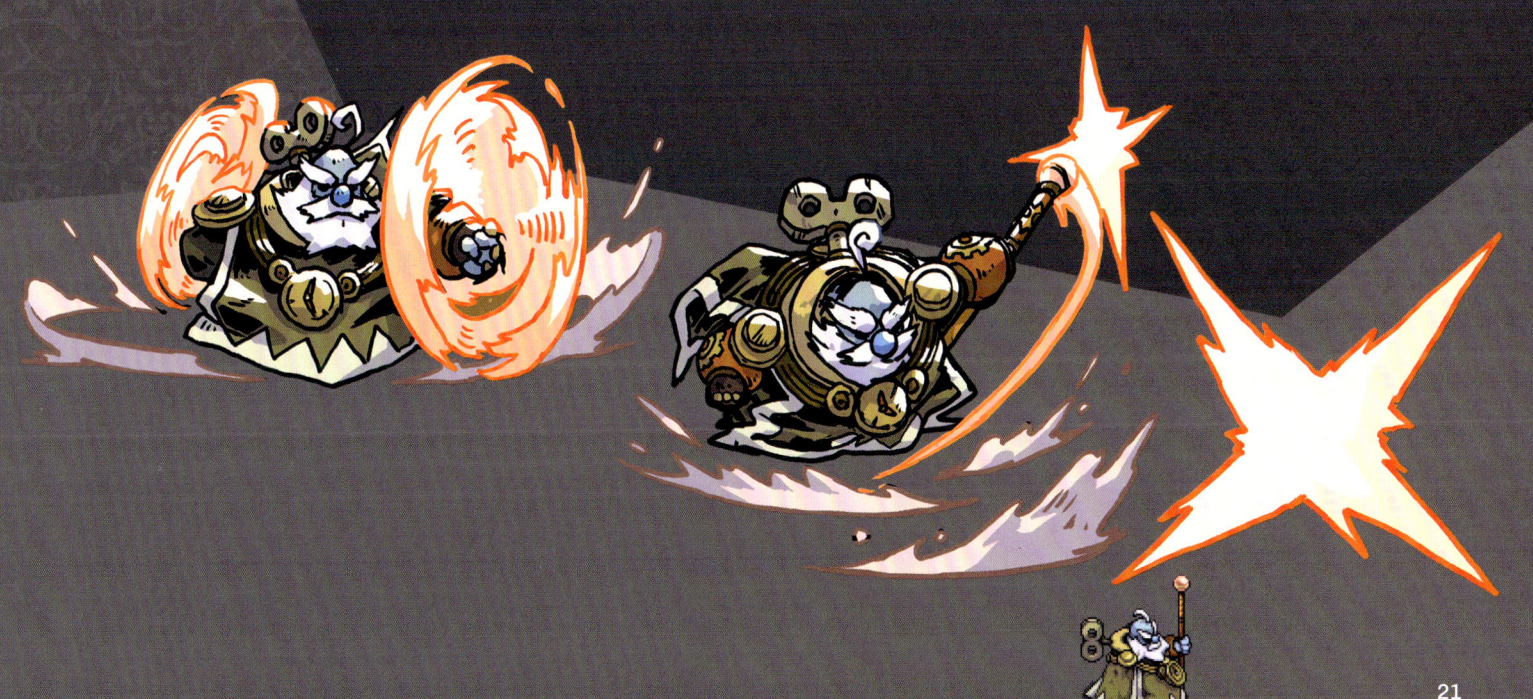

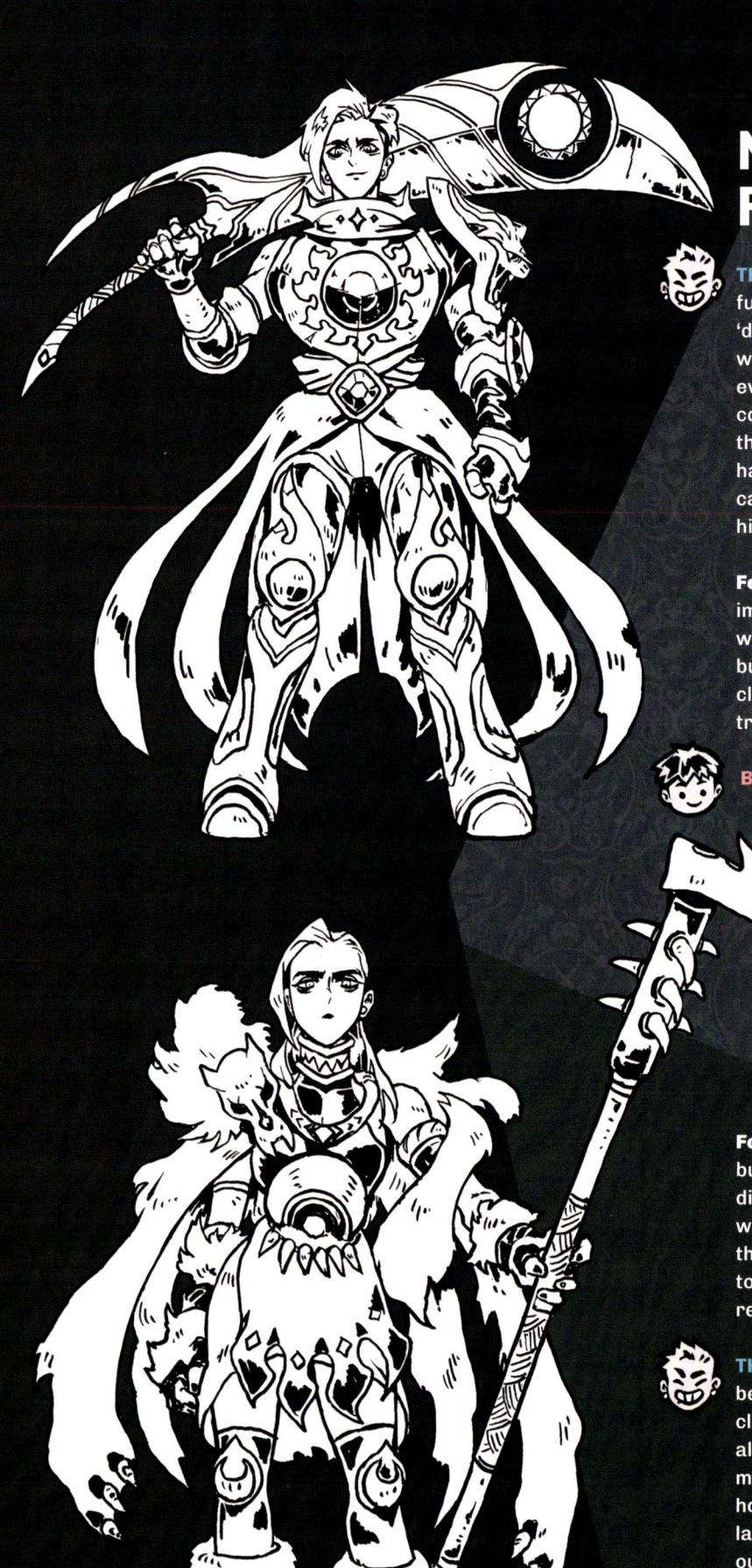

Narcis King Zale & Feral Queen Valere

THIERRY: Narcis King Zale – I think this one should be fun! What we need here could also be summarized as 'douchebag Zale'. He is a deluded sun god who believes what his believers do, which is that he is the best thing ever. He is obsessed with himself and his looks. It would be cool to see some special-move ideas, too. Two references that come to mind here are *BOF3*'s adult Ryu for the cool hair and white jacket, and Jaime Lannister for the white cape, haughty demeanor, and the way his hand rests on his sword. Unlike everyone else, he's not clockwork.

Feral Queen Valere – I think this intro is very easy to imagine, where she sits atop World Rock on a stone throne with the full moon in the background. It's not mandatory, but I can't help imagining her with short hair and fighting claws. All up to you, as long as we get a good feral/tribalistic spin on Valere! She's not clockwork, either.

BRYCE: These two drafts are pretty much my first impressions, and sometimes that's what you're most into, too, so I figured I'd just show these first before doing any other alternatives. For both designs, I tried to keep the overall motifs the same, especially where their solstice garments stood out most.

For Zale, I imagine his spirit animal and alternative form would be a golden lion, since that seems like the most kingly and sun-aligned animal.

For Valere, I know you mentioned short hair and claws, but when I tried it out, she just looked like a completely different character. I don't mind trying again if you really want to see it, but that would mean I'd mostly have to keep their 'baby' good-guy faces. I think most players will want to see as much contrast as possible for these alternate-reality versions.

THIERRY: I absolutely love these! That being said, it'll be hard for me to give up on the 'short hair + Wolverine claws' idea, so I think it'd be worth pursuing if only to allow my stubborn brain to say 'OK, it doesn't work, let's move on.' Also, I don't think there'll be a bottleneck given how the rest is going so far. We can do these two bosses last if that's what makes sense. I'd say it's worth taking our time and trying options, if only as a sanity check. They'll be the stars, so let's go to town. Please don't worry about time (at least in regards to the team here).

BRYCE: Zale & Valere with alternative weapons – I tried to follow your request as closely as possible for Valere while still making her recognizable to a degree. Notice how the animal versions of each character are more ingrained into their outfits with the wolf and lion heads hiding in plain sight.

For Zale, I went with more of an arrogant douche as opposed to the egotistical look of the previous iteration. This is a self-important, 'I AM RIGHTEOUS/I AM THE LAW' vibe, which might be a good contrast from Valere's 'I'm a rebel who doesn't care' attitude. My feeling is that the ego Zale could hit a similar note, so this is an option for contrast if you don't want them to be as closely team-oriented like the last set. Zale's weapon is a big sunball mace, haha. One more detail to point out is that I managed to make the cogs part of their outfits as well (shoulder pad for Zale, belt for Valere), which is a nice touch given their origin as clockwork-born.

 THIERRY: So, here are my thoughts in summary, happy to get more in-detail about anything:

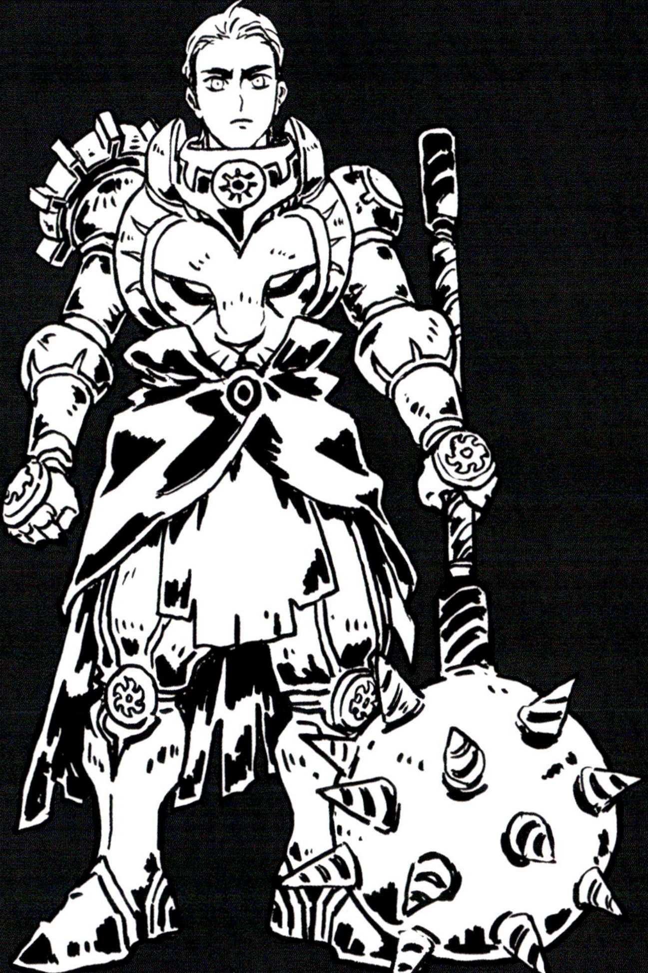

Zale #1 – Love the pose, haughtiness, sword, and the dark around the eyes.

Zale #2 – Love everything about the armour, but head and weapon of option A are it, IMO. The big morning star takes it too far away from Zale (making him go from agility to strength, I feel), but the size and idea are absolutely amazing, so I'm crossing my fingers someone in his kingsguard can have that as a weapon.

Valere #1 – I love option B too much to be able to properly speak to this one, but I feel like we should keep her boots!

Valere #2 – Other than the boots, she's honestly what I was hoping for. But sitting with it for a while got me thinking that, for consistency's sake, we might want her to have a staff tucked behind her back, still leading with claws but maybe finishing combos with it from time to time. Also, it's mostly the hair that I'm really into. I know you mentioned that making it shorter would mean the face has to feel more familiar, and I can appreciate that, but I also can't shake the feeling that the face from option A would be stronger. I don't know if there's an in-between here where it looks more like her while keeping the evil expression and dark around the eyes.

 BRYCE: Hmm, so for Zale you mostly prefer option A and for Valere you mostly prefer option B, perhaps with some borrowed elements (armour from B for Zale, boots from A for Valere).

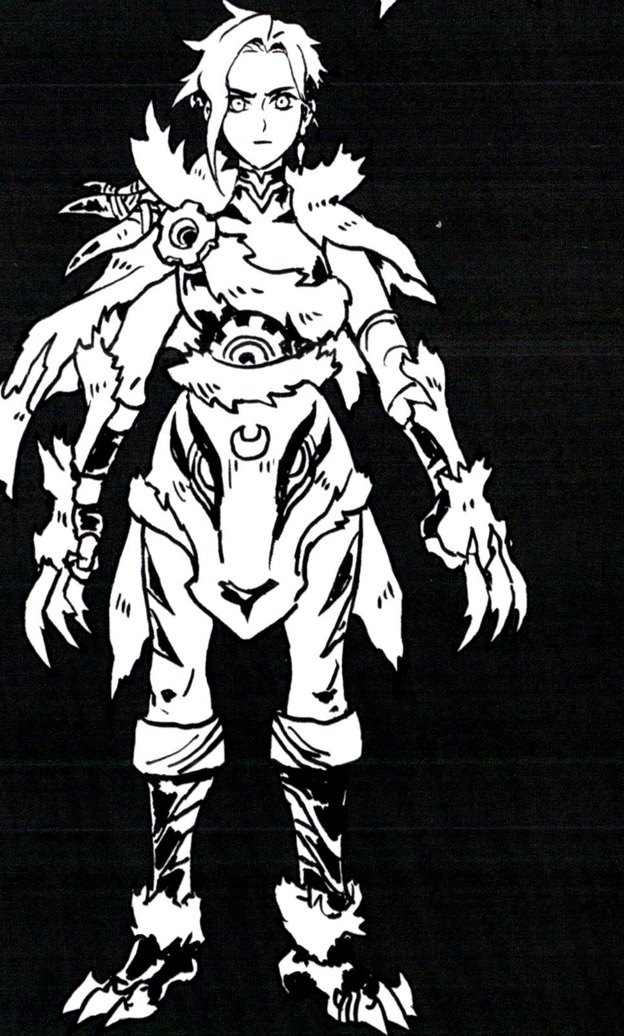

For Valere's hair, I mostly stand by the idea that if we change both the face and hair, it basically becomes a different character. But I am willing to try another pass at both characters with the tweaks you mentioned to see if that changes anything for me. I'll try a sassier, short-haired Valere, lol.

 THIERRY: Haha, right. As far as the either/or goes, I'm more partial to the hair being shorter. But yeah, this was a tough one.

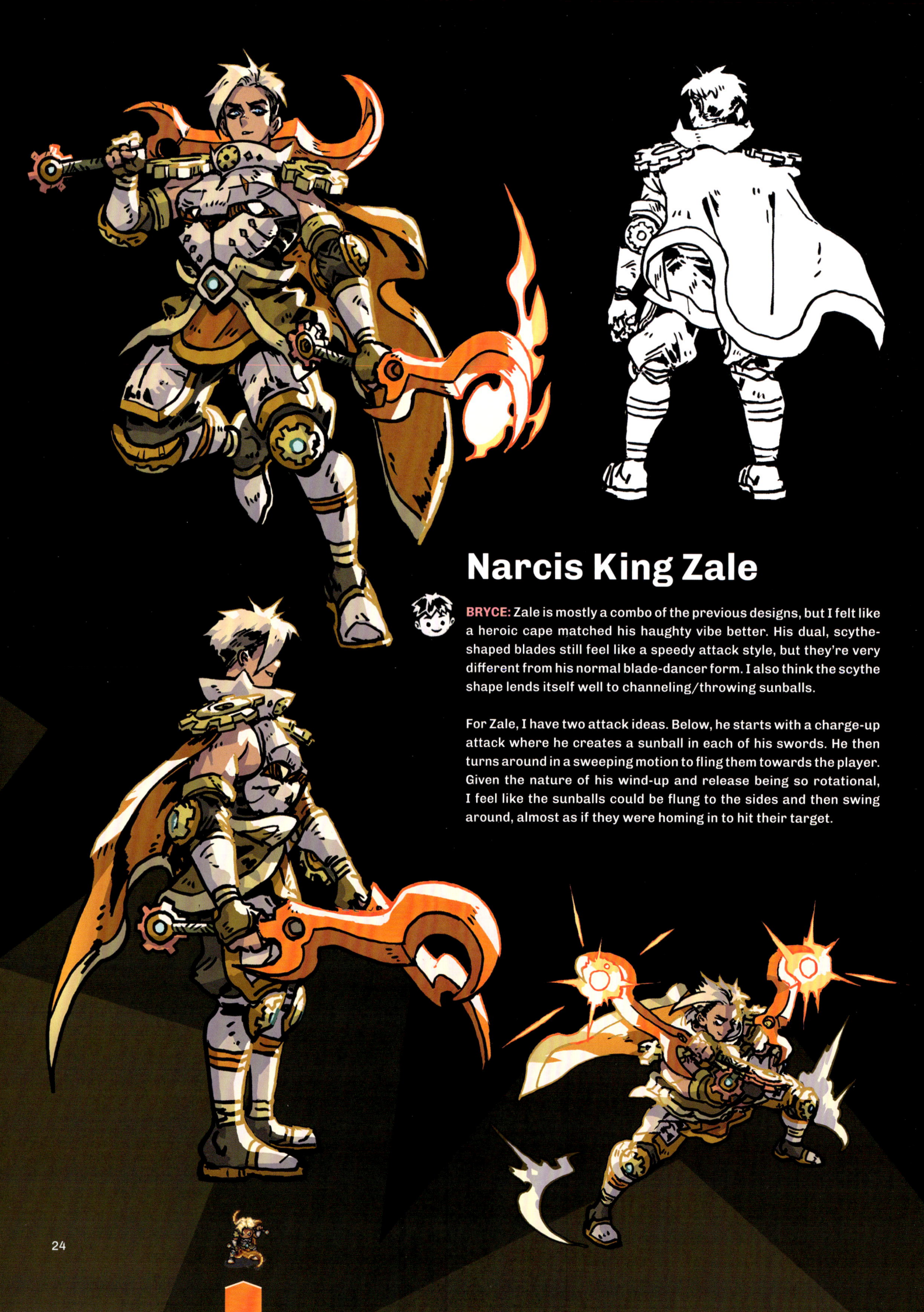

Narcis King Zale

BRYCE: Zale is mostly a combo of the previous designs, but I felt like a heroic cape matched his haughty vibe better. His dual, scythe-shaped blades still feel like a speedy attack style, but they're very different from his normal blade-dancer form. I also think the scythe shape lends itself well to channeling/throwing sunballs.

For Zale, I have two attack ideas. Below, he starts with a charge-up attack where he creates a sunball in each of his swords. He then turns around in a sweeping motion to fling them towards the player. Given the nature of his wind-up and release being so rotational, I feel like the sunballs could be flung to the sides and then swing around, almost as if they were homing in to hit their target.

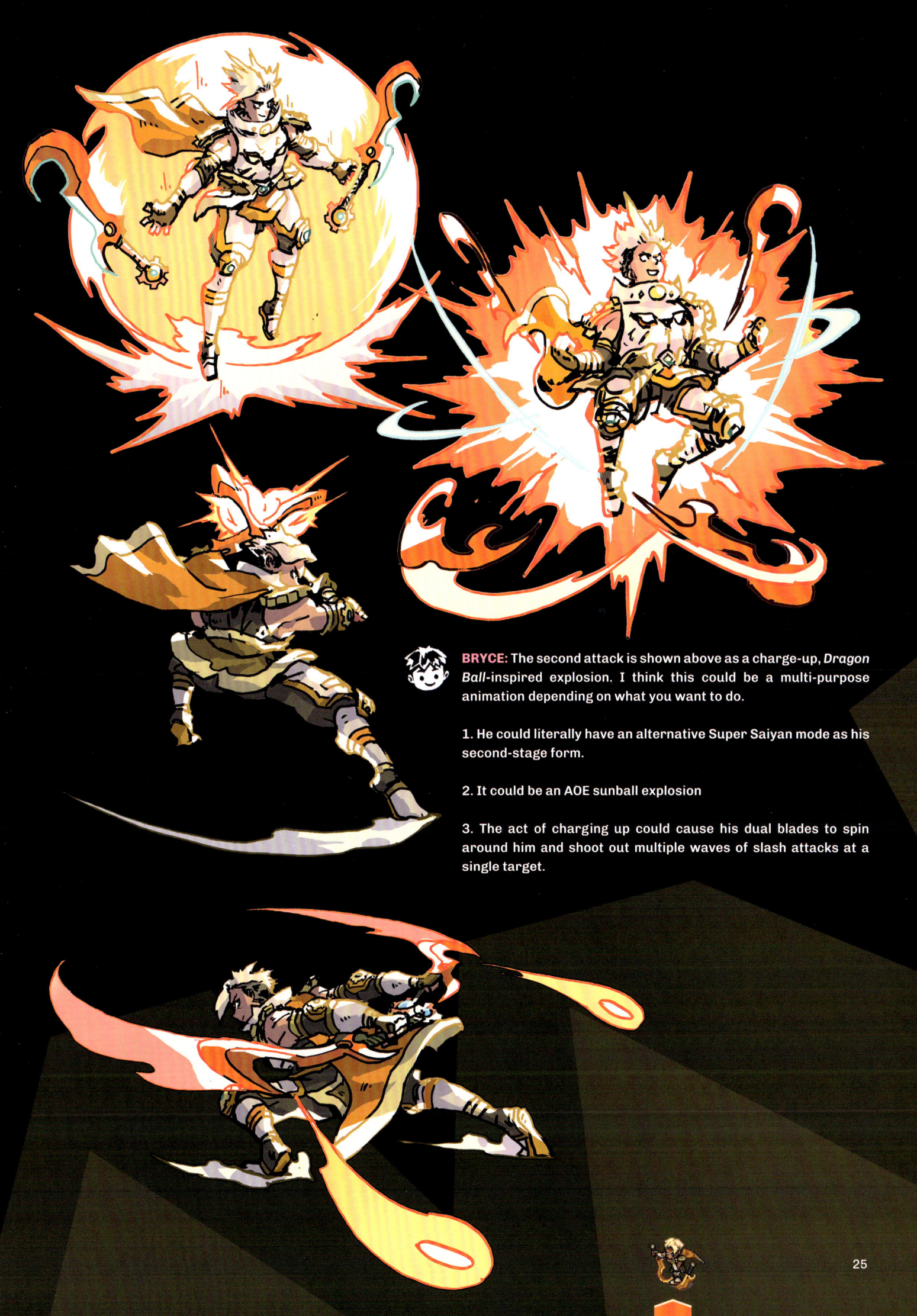

BRYCE: The second attack is shown above as a charge-up, *Dragon Ball*-inspired explosion. I think this could be a multi-purpose animation depending on what you want to do.

1. He could literally have an alternative Super Saiyan mode as his second-stage form.

2. It could be an AOE sunball explosion

3. The act of charging up could cause his dual blades to spin around him and shoot out multiple waves of slash attacks at a single target.

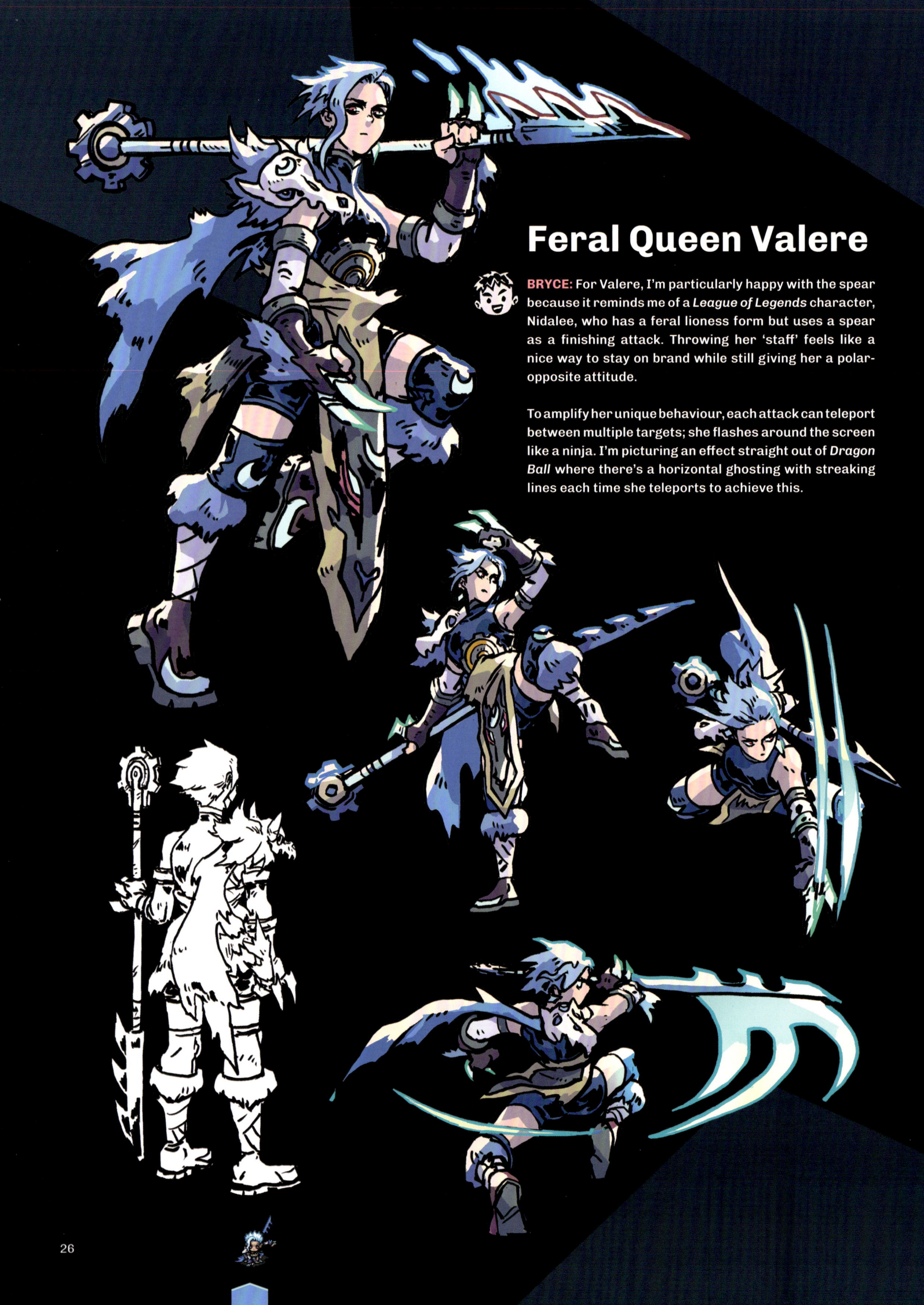

Feral Queen Valere

BRYCE: For Valere, I'm particularly happy with the spear because it reminds me of a *League of Legends* character, Nidalee, who has a feral lioness form but uses a spear as a finishing attack. Throwing her 'staff' feels like a nice way to stay on brand while still giving her a polar-opposite attitude.

To amplify her unique behaviour, each attack can teleport between multiple targets; she flashes around the screen like a ninja. I'm picturing an effect straight out of *Dragon Ball* where there's a horizontal ghosting with streaking lines each time she teleports to achieve this.

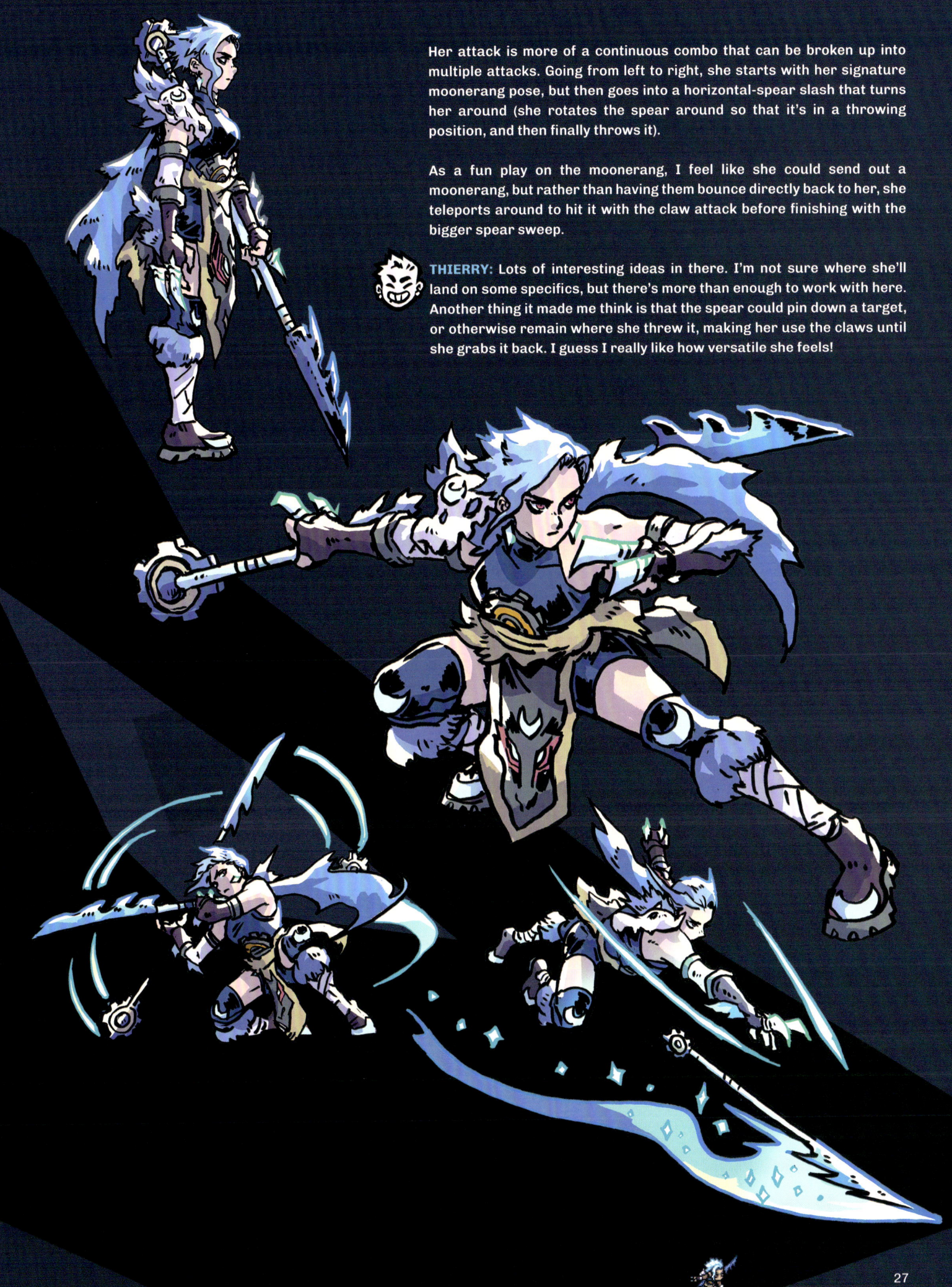

Her attack is more of a continuous combo that can be broken up into multiple attacks. Going from left to right, she starts with her signature moonerang pose, but then goes into a horizontal-spear slash that turns her around (she rotates the spear around so that it's in a throwing position, and then finally throws it).

As a fun play on the moonerang, I feel like she could send out a moonerang, but rather than having them bounce directly back to her, she teleports around to hit it with the claw attack before finishing with the bigger spear sweep.

THIERRY: Lots of interesting ideas in there. I'm not sure where she'll land on some specifics, but there's more than enough to work with here. Another thing it made me think is that the spear could pin down a target, or otherwise remain where she threw it, making her use the claws until she grabs it back. I guess I really like how versatile she feels!

Werewolf Enemies

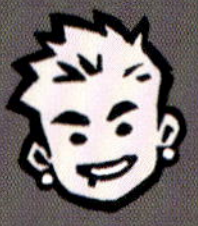

 THIERRY: Much like the previous dungeon, we need a balanced set of 'crazed followers' for Evil Valere. I don't think we can go wrong with werewolves, though it might be interesting to see some transformations happening during the fights. Clockwork here again, with some circus attacks, too. I suppose a werewolf on a unicycle is a good start, lol.

 BRYCE: Werewolf Bruiser – Pretty much on-prompt for a strong melee attacker with glowing moon glyphs to spice up the design. Just like with Zale's clockwork enemies, notice the dopey clockwork nose, somewhat hidden to keep them cool while maintaining that consistency.

Wolf Hunter – *Mononoke*-style spear hunter wearing wolf fur to join the club.

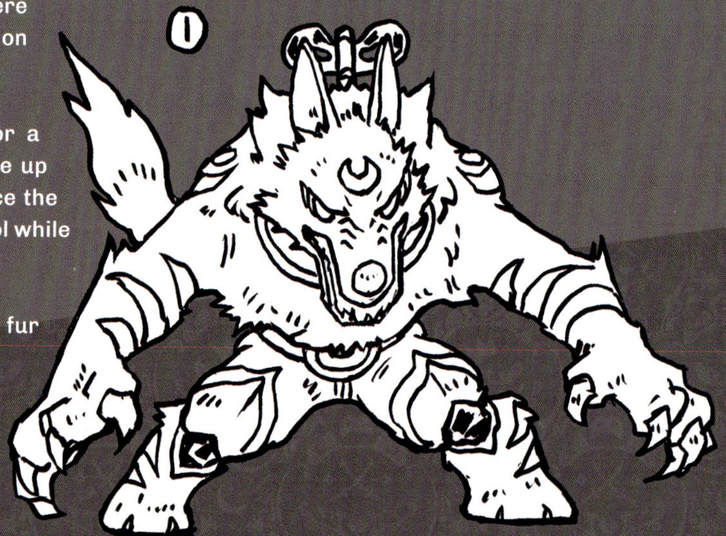

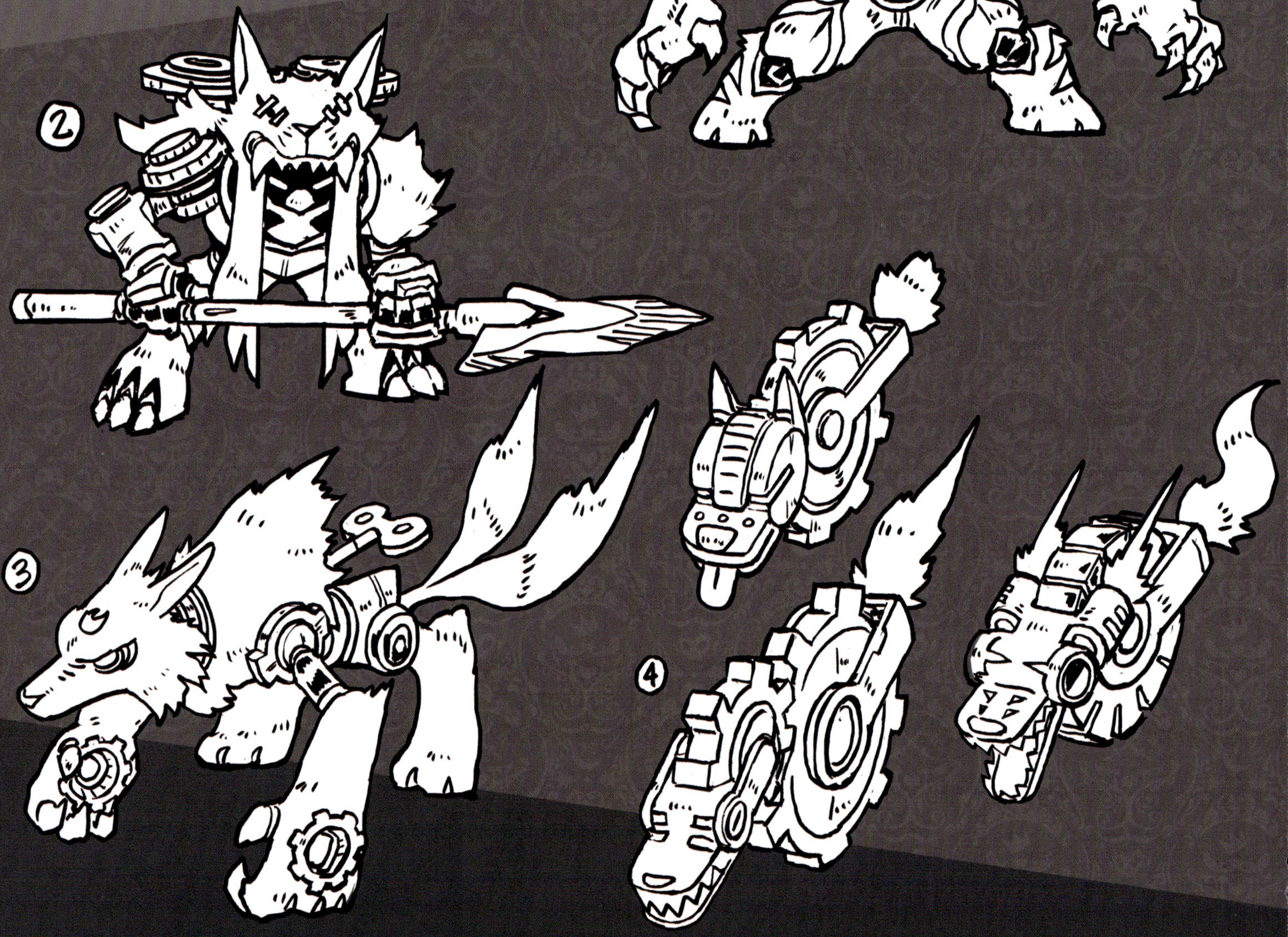

Clockwork Wolf – The same spiritual concept as #1 but with a more natural/conventional wolf body. Between #1 and #3, I think it's more down to whether you want to keep Valere's ability to transform into a wolf a unique surprise, or if it should be something we're looking forward to seeing.

Cog Wolf Pack – Notice how their tails will look like the flame exhaust on a motorcycle. At first I wasn't sure how it would attack. When I added the other two, it made more sense that they would just hop around/roll into the player as a fun timing challenge for the player to block. I also fully expect the dumb pupper on the top to sometimes lick you or chase after its own tail.

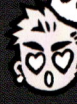 **THIERRY:** You had me at *Mononoke* before I even read your words. So, Wolf Hunter is a must-have, and I feel Bruiser is the strong 'hit the nail on the head' one we need. So, #1 and #2 here as well! I'm thinking since #4 might be simpler to illustrate, it could be worth exploring too, but I'll defer to you!

Wolf Bruiser

BRYCE: A big awooooo howl. This could be a self-buff, a supersonic ranged attack, or a call capable of a few things. I have a semi-crazy idea that the other hunter enemy can turn into the werewolf. So, this animation can be used to trigger the transformation of any other hunters on the battlefield.

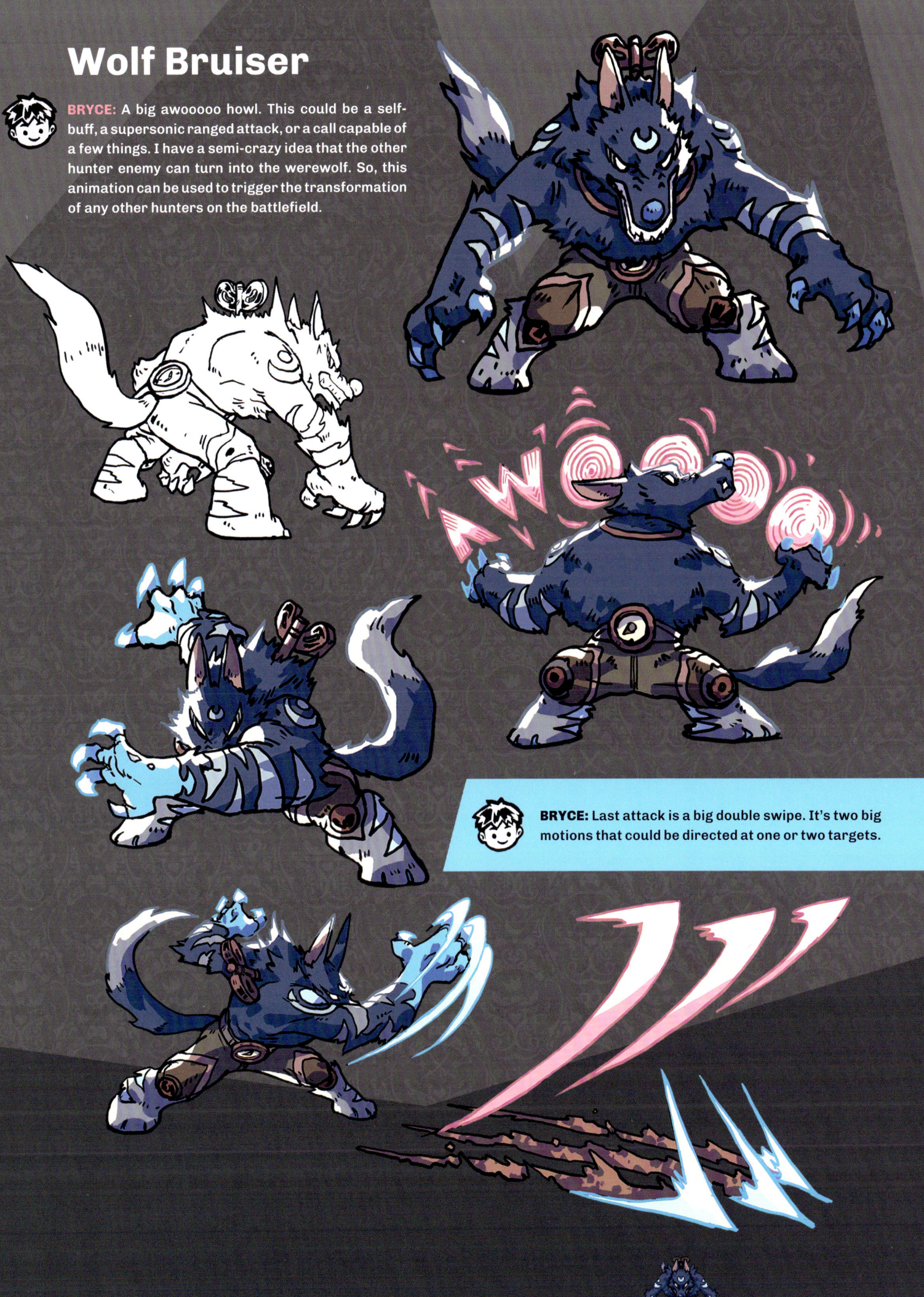

AWOOO

BRYCE: Last attack is a big double swipe. It's two big motions that could be directed at one or two targets.

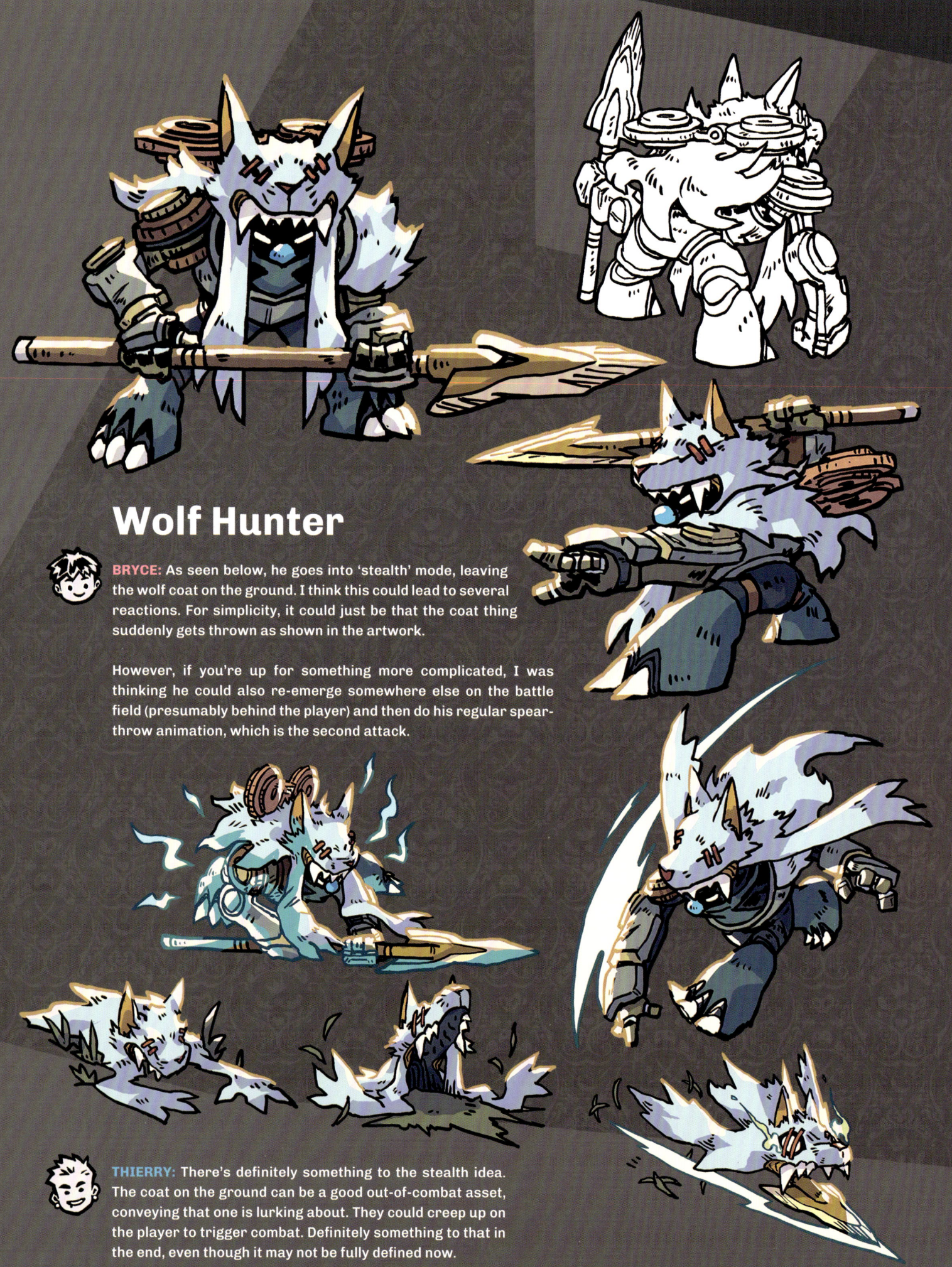

Wolf Hunter

BRYCE: As seen below, he goes into 'stealth' mode, leaving the wolf coat on the ground. I think this could lead to several reactions. For simplicity, it could just be that the coat thing suddenly gets thrown as shown in the artwork.

However, if you're up for something more complicated, I was thinking he could also re-emerge somewhere else on the battle field (presumably behind the player) and then do his regular spear-throw animation, which is the second attack.

THIERRY: There's definitely something to the stealth idea. The coat on the ground can be a good out-of-combat asset, conveying that one is lurking about. They could creep up on the player to trigger combat. Definitely something to that in the end, even though it may not be fully defined now.

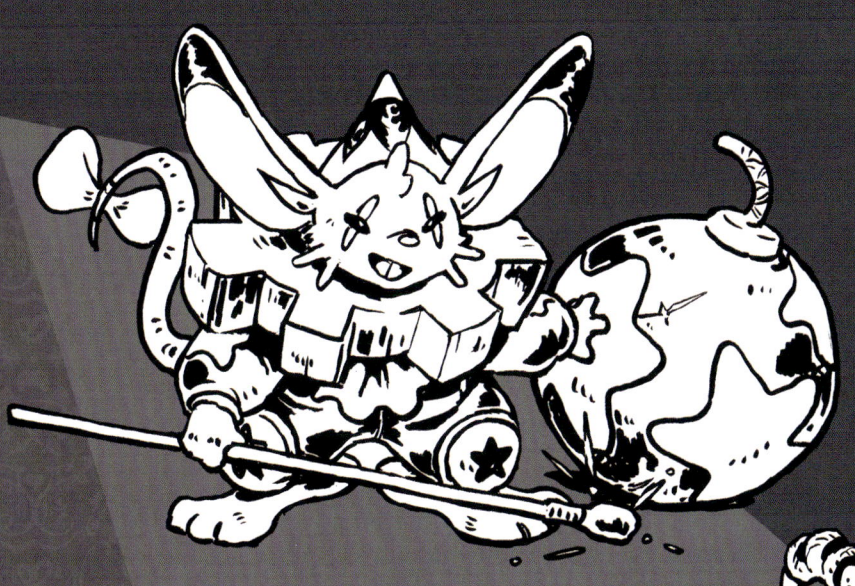

Chapiteau Enemies

 THIERRY: Since the place will be lightly reusing the previous enemies and mostly focuses on boss fights, we only need two varieties here. The idea would be for them to be minions of Pif & Pouf, so clowns of sorts, with their attacks centering around circus moves.

 BRYCE: **Mouse Bombadier & Key Maker** – Reusing the designs for the bodies on these mice guys, but with different purposes. For the Bombadier, he uses a giant matchstick to light bombs before kicking them at the player. I'm wondering if the bomb has a separate countdown timer for when it explodes? I think the Key Maker could still use it to trigger things falling on the player/trap doors or to heal/speed up other clockwork enemies.

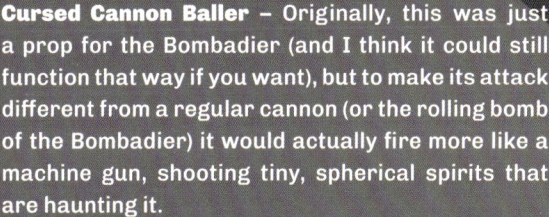

Cursed Cannon Baller – Originally, this was just a prop for the Bombadier (and I think it could still function that way if you want), but to make its attack different from a regular cannon (or the rolling bomb of the Bombadier) it would actually fire more like a machine gun, shooting tiny, spherical spirits that are haunting it.

Pig Cog Lifter – I wanted to design a heavy clockwork enemy. Pretty straightforward, but I think he'd be a nice change of pace for the more mechanically complex ideas in this act.

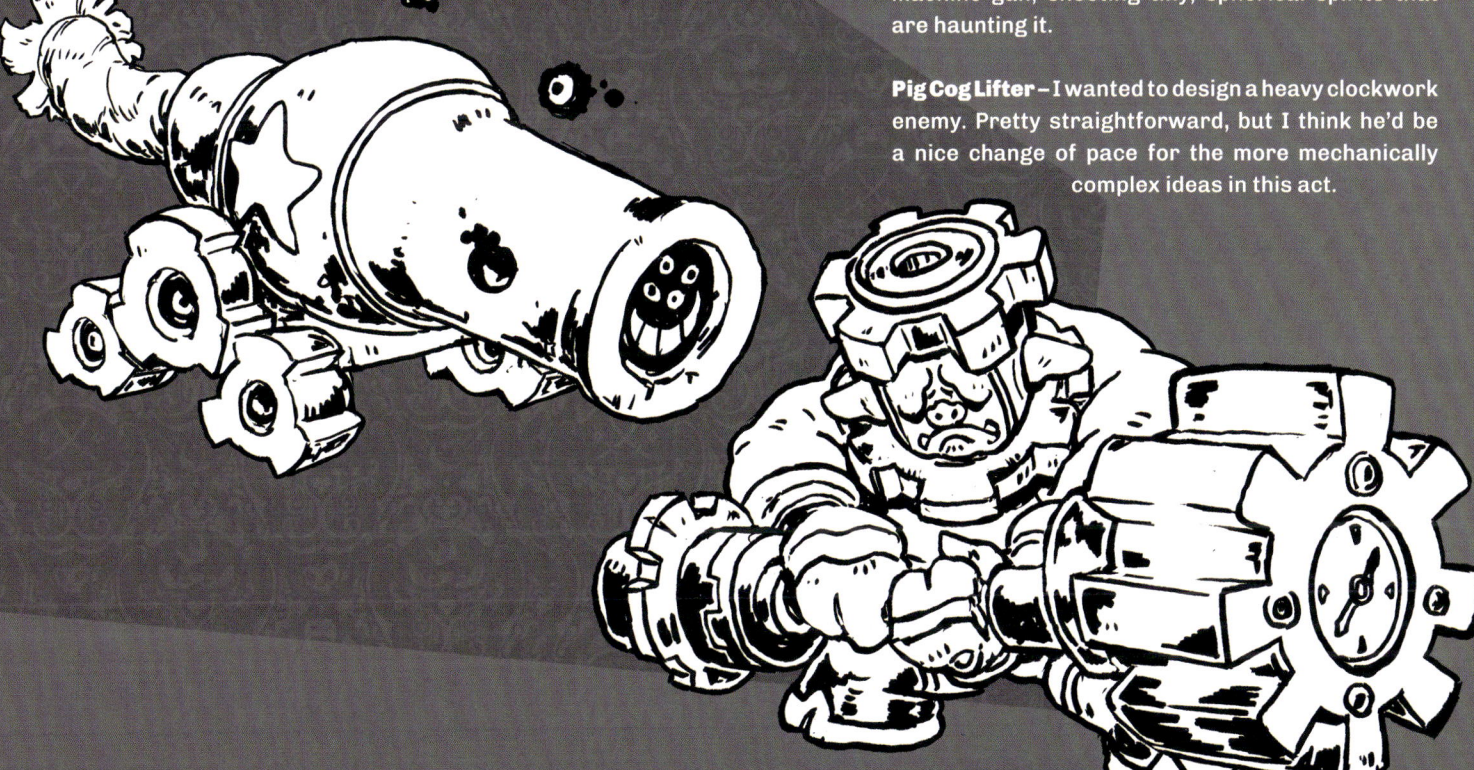

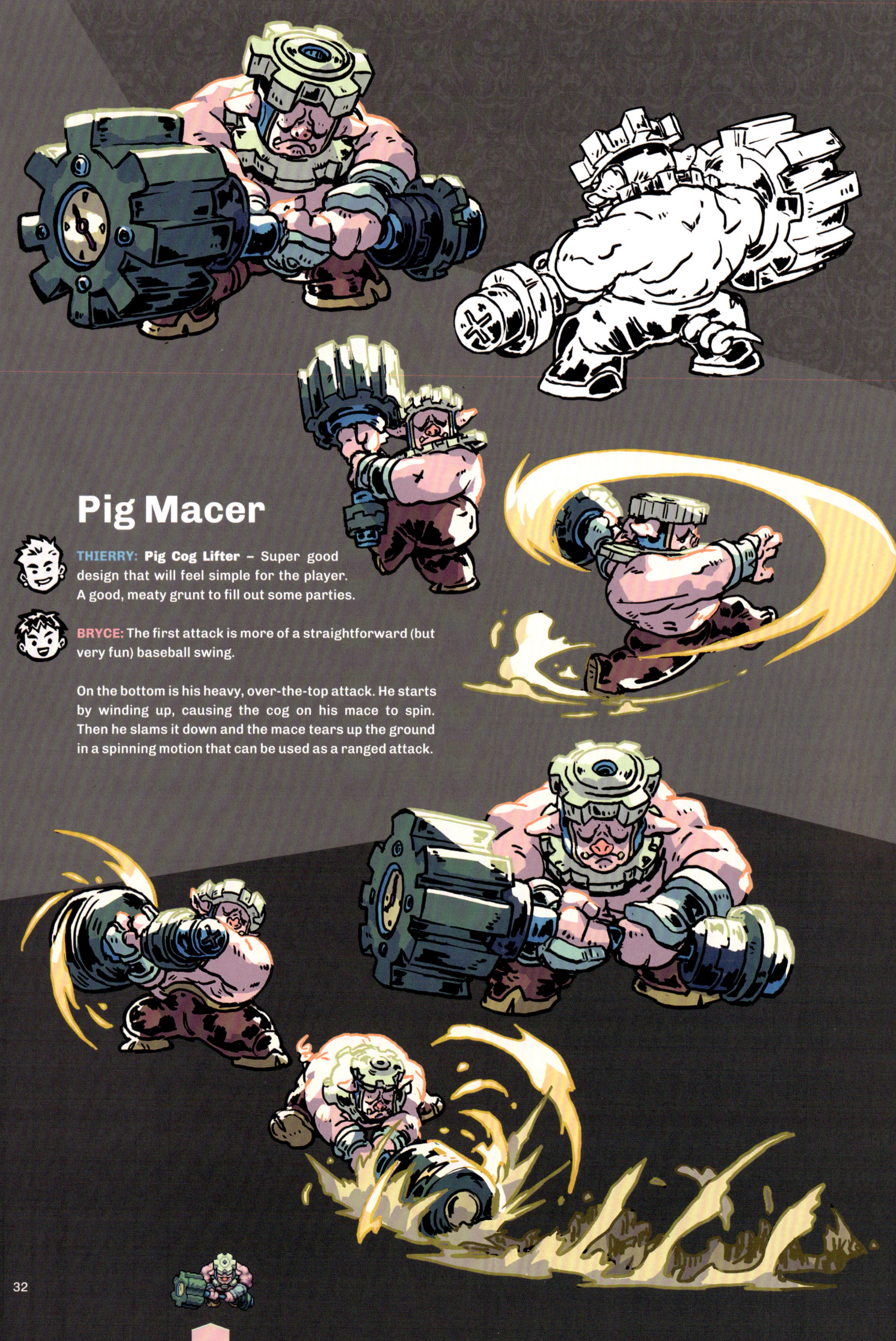

Pig Macer

THIERRY: Pig Cog Lifter – Super good design that will feel simple for the player. A good, meaty grunt to fill out some parties.

BRYCE: The first attack is more of a straightforward (but very fun) baseball swing.

On the bottom is his heavy, over-the-top attack. He starts by winding up, causing the cog on his mace to spin. Then he slams it down and the mace tears up the ground in a spinning motion that can be used as a ranged attack.

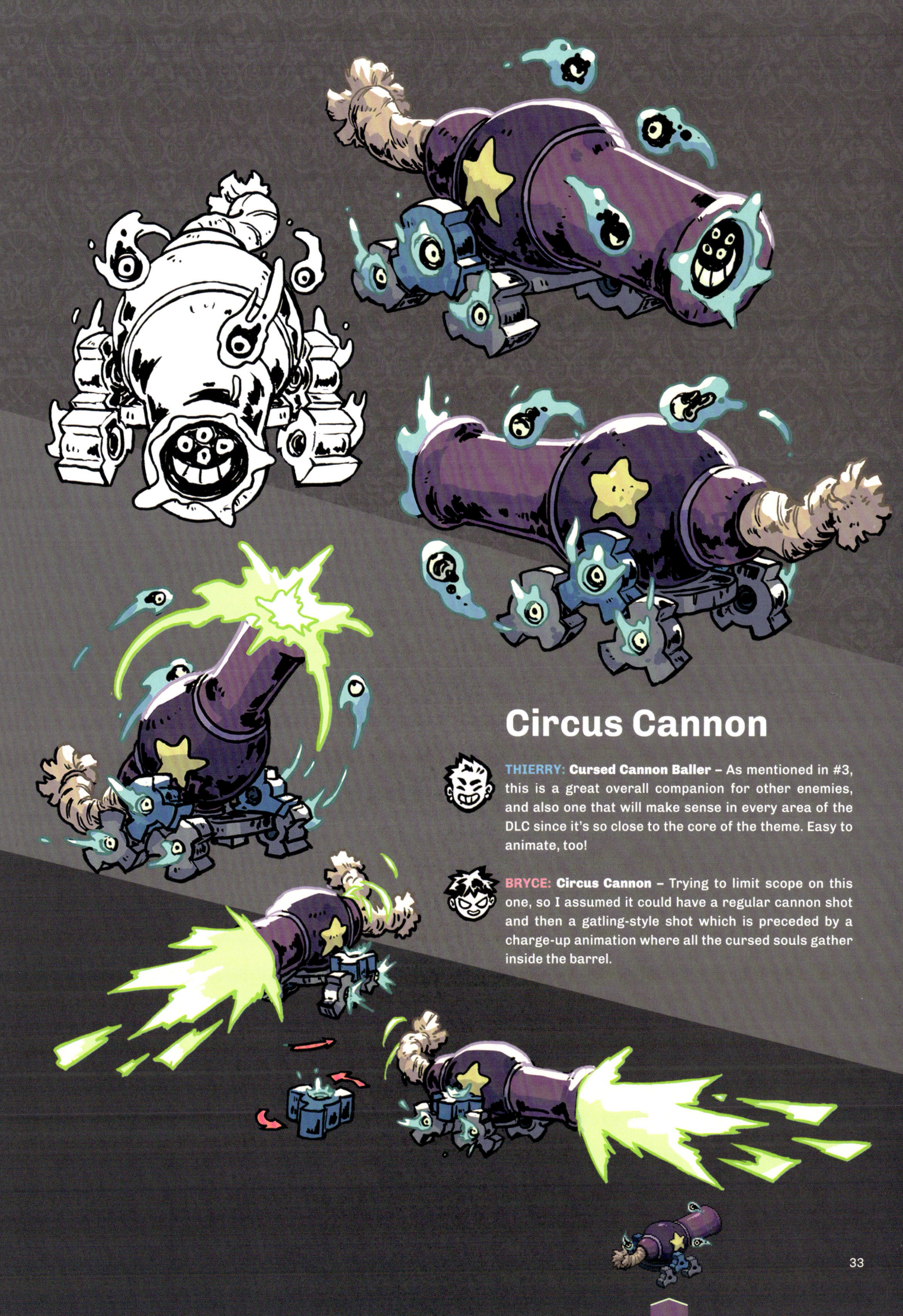

Circus Cannon

THIERRY: Cursed Cannon Baller – As mentioned in #3, this is a great overall companion for other enemies, and also one that will make sense in every area of the DLC since it's so close to the core of the theme. Easy to animate, too!

BRYCE: Circus Cannon – Trying to limit scope on this one, so I assumed it could have a regular cannon shot and then a gatling-style shot which is preceded by a charge-up animation where all the cursed souls gather inside the barrel.

Mice Bombardiers

 THIERRY: I'm also thinking we'll give them some synergies, not that they have to come as a pair, but that if they happen to be together in a fight, the Key Master could unlock something the Bombardier ignites for more power. Or, conversely, he uses his keys to tinker with the big bomb to unlock more explosive potential.

They could also both interact with the cursed cannon. This idea of dynamically creating combos between the enemies is growing on me after seeing these!

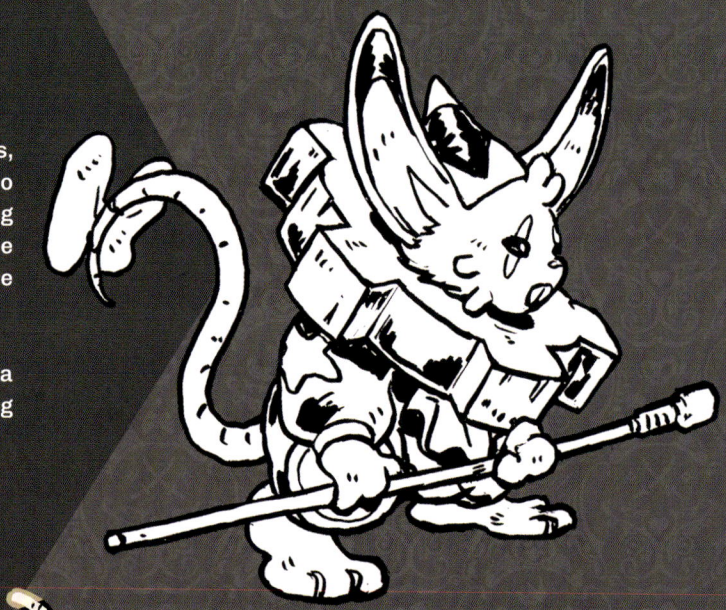

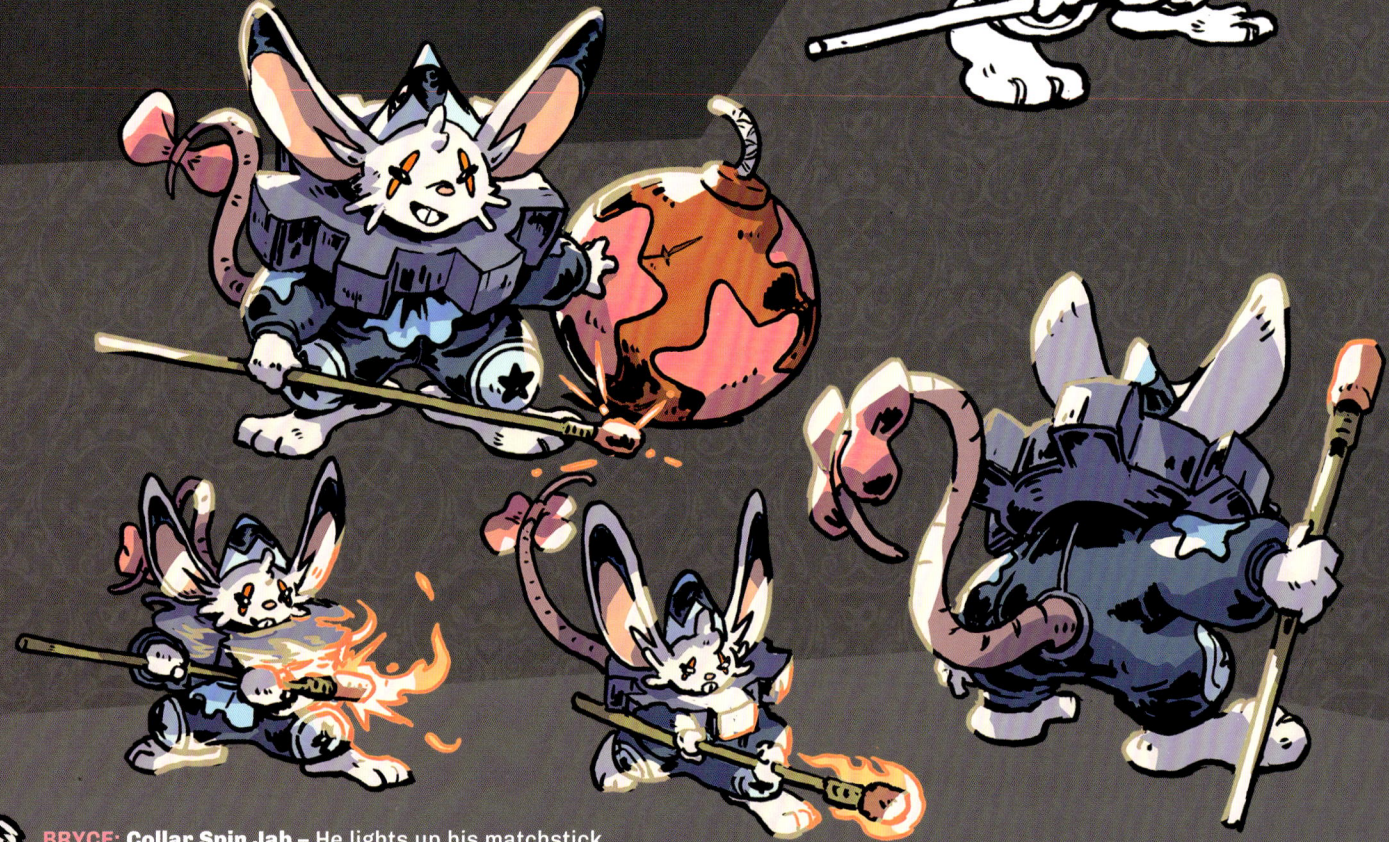

 BRYCE: Collar Spin Jab – He lights up his matchstick by striking it with the cog around his neck, which spins. Lastly, a jab to either attack the player or light bombs.

Bomb Dance – He waves his matchstick in the air and spins around to make unlit bombs fall from the sky.

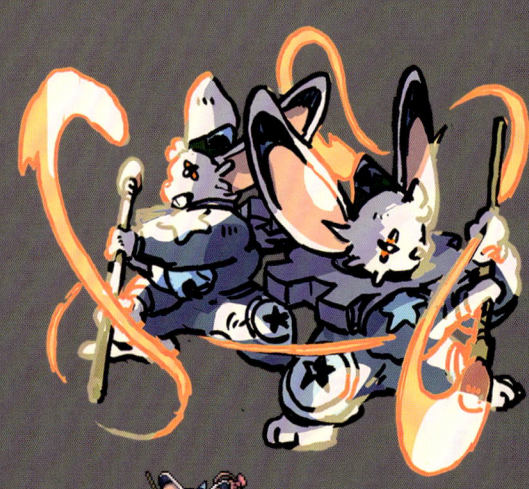

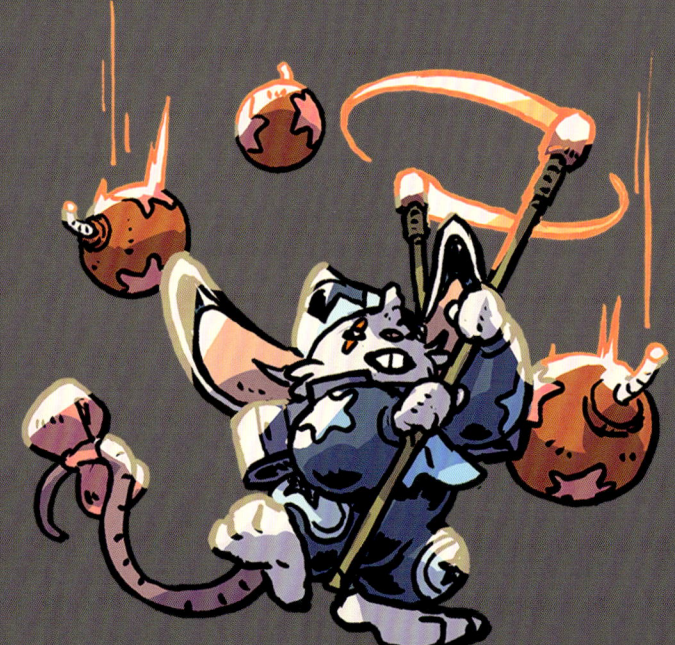

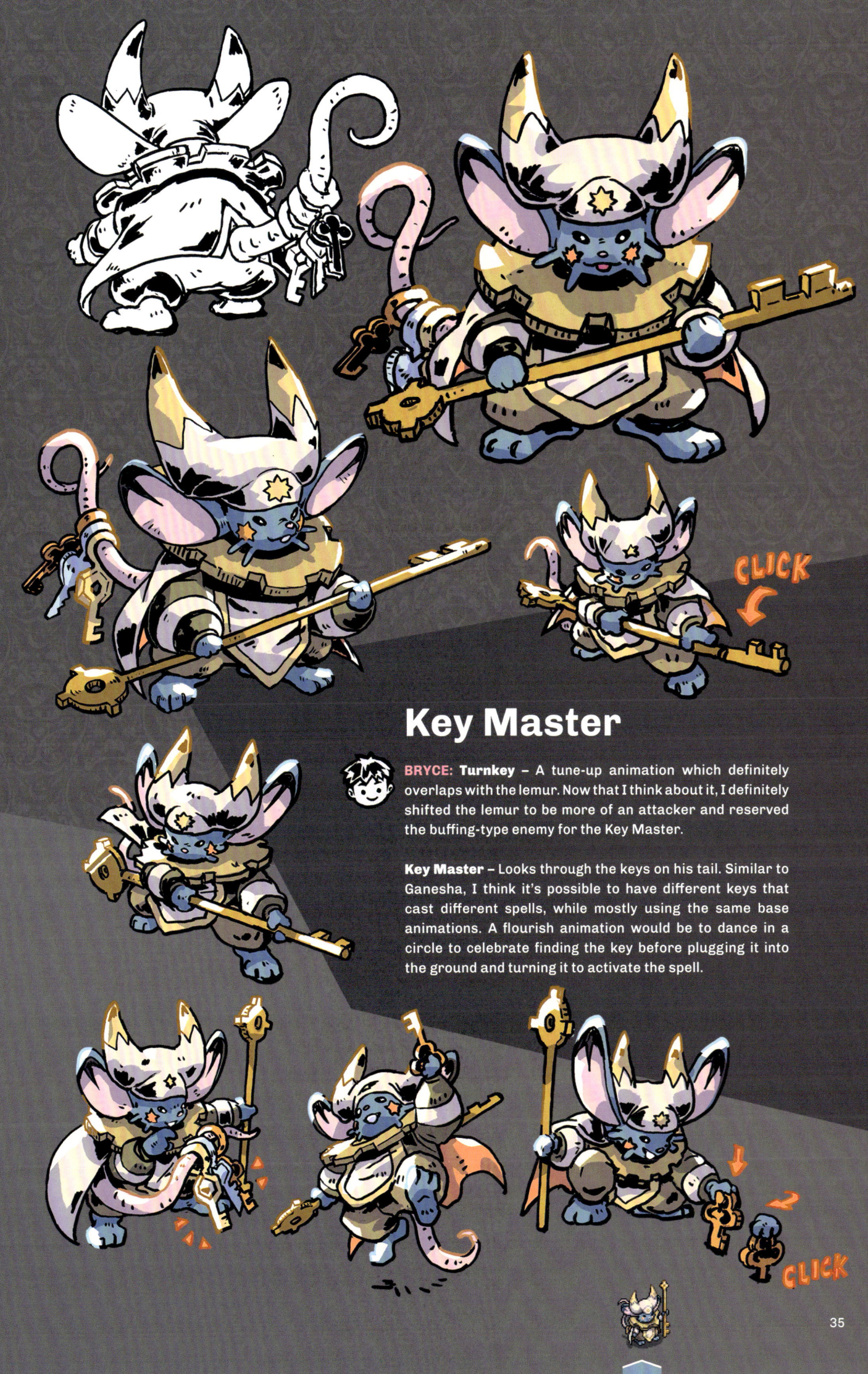

Key Master

BRYCE: Turnkey – A tune-up animation which definitely overlaps with the lemur. Now that I think about it, I definitely shifted the lemur to be more of an attacker and reserved the buffing-type enemy for the Key Master.

Key Master – Looks through the keys on his tail. Similar to Ganesha, I think it's possible to have different keys that cast different spells, while mostly using the same base animations. A flourish animation would be to dance in a circle to celebrate finding the key before plugging it into the ground and turning it to activate the spell.

CLICK

CLICK

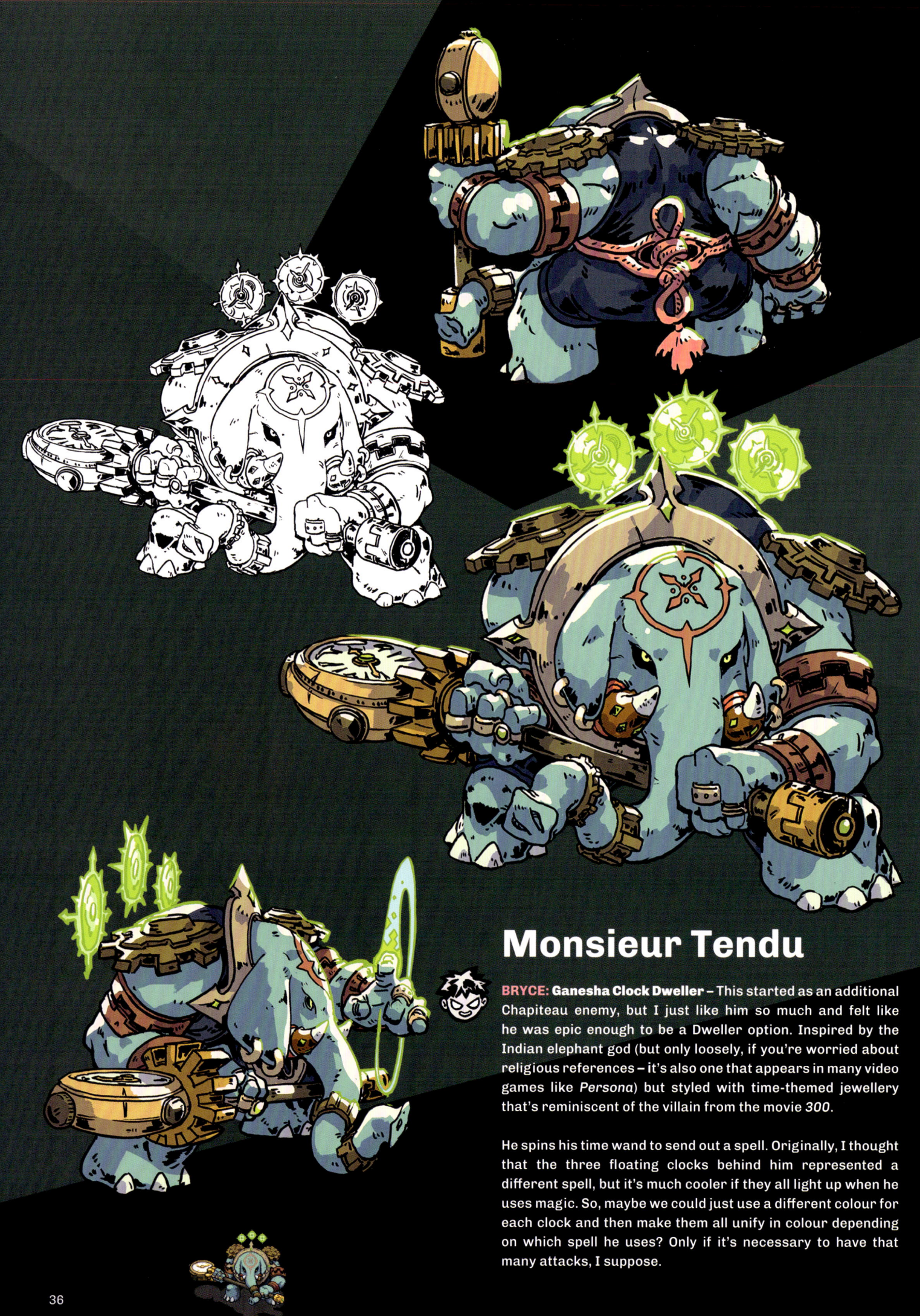

Monsieur Tendu

BRYCE: Ganesha Clock Dweller – This started as an additional Chapiteau enemy, but I just like him so much and felt like he was epic enough to be a Dweller option. Inspired by the Indian elephant god (but only loosely, if you're worried about religious references – it's also one that appears in many video games like *Persona*) but styled with time-themed jewellery that's reminiscent of the villain from the movie *300*.

He spins his time wand to send out a spell. Originally, I thought that the three floating clocks behind him represented a different spell, but it's much cooler if they all light up when he uses magic. So, maybe we could just use a different colour for each clock and then make them all unify in colour depending on which spell he uses? Only if it's necessary to have that many attacks, I suppose.

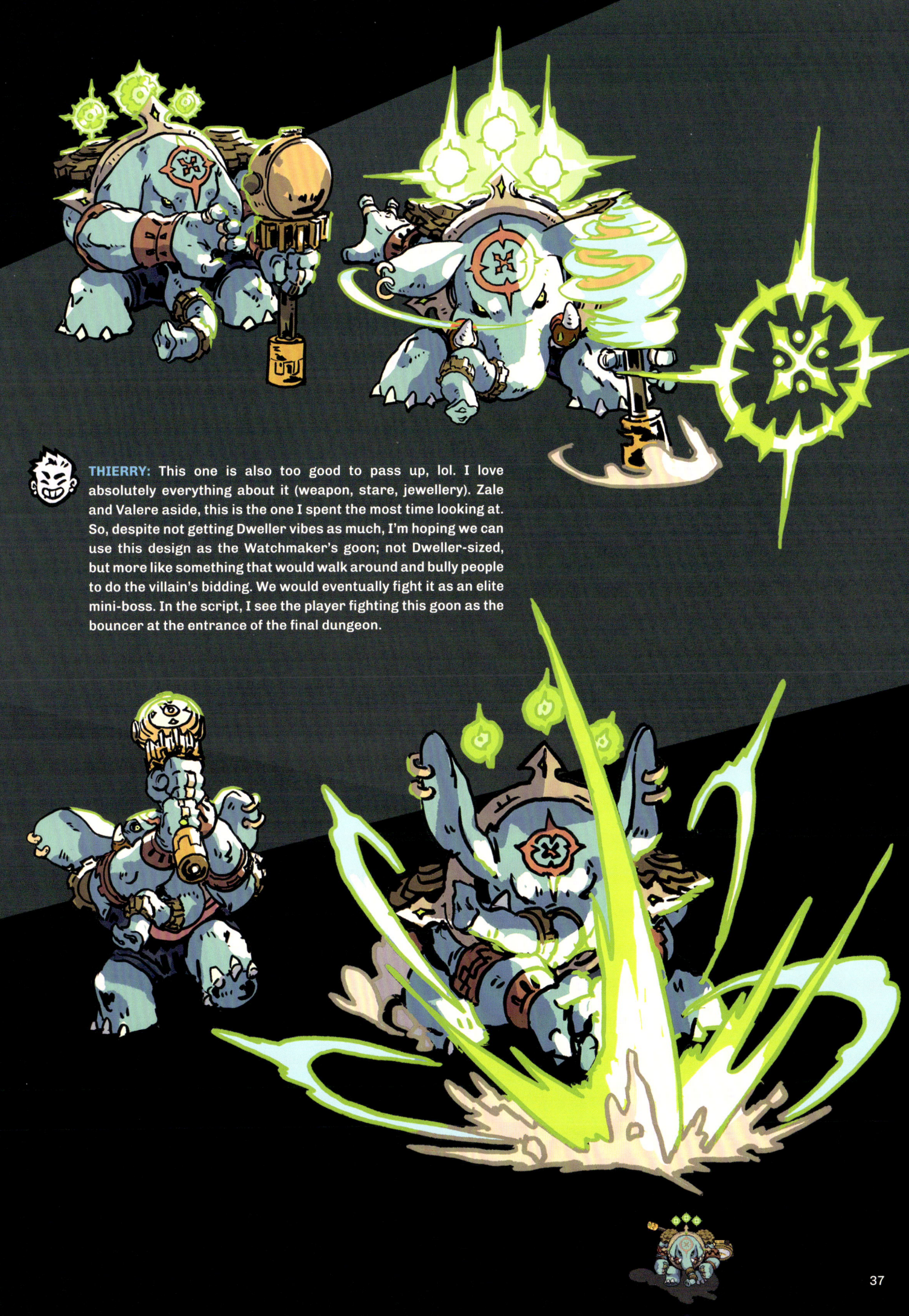

THIERRY: This one is also too good to pass up, lol. I love absolutely everything about it (weapon, stare, jewellery). Zale and Valere aside, this is the one I spent the most time looking at. So, despite not getting Dweller vibes as much, I'm hoping we can use this design as the Watchmaker's goon; not Dweller-sized, but more like something that would walk around and bully people to do the villain's bidding. We would eventually fight it as an elite mini-boss. In the script, I see the player fighting this goon as the bouncer at the entrance of the final dungeon.

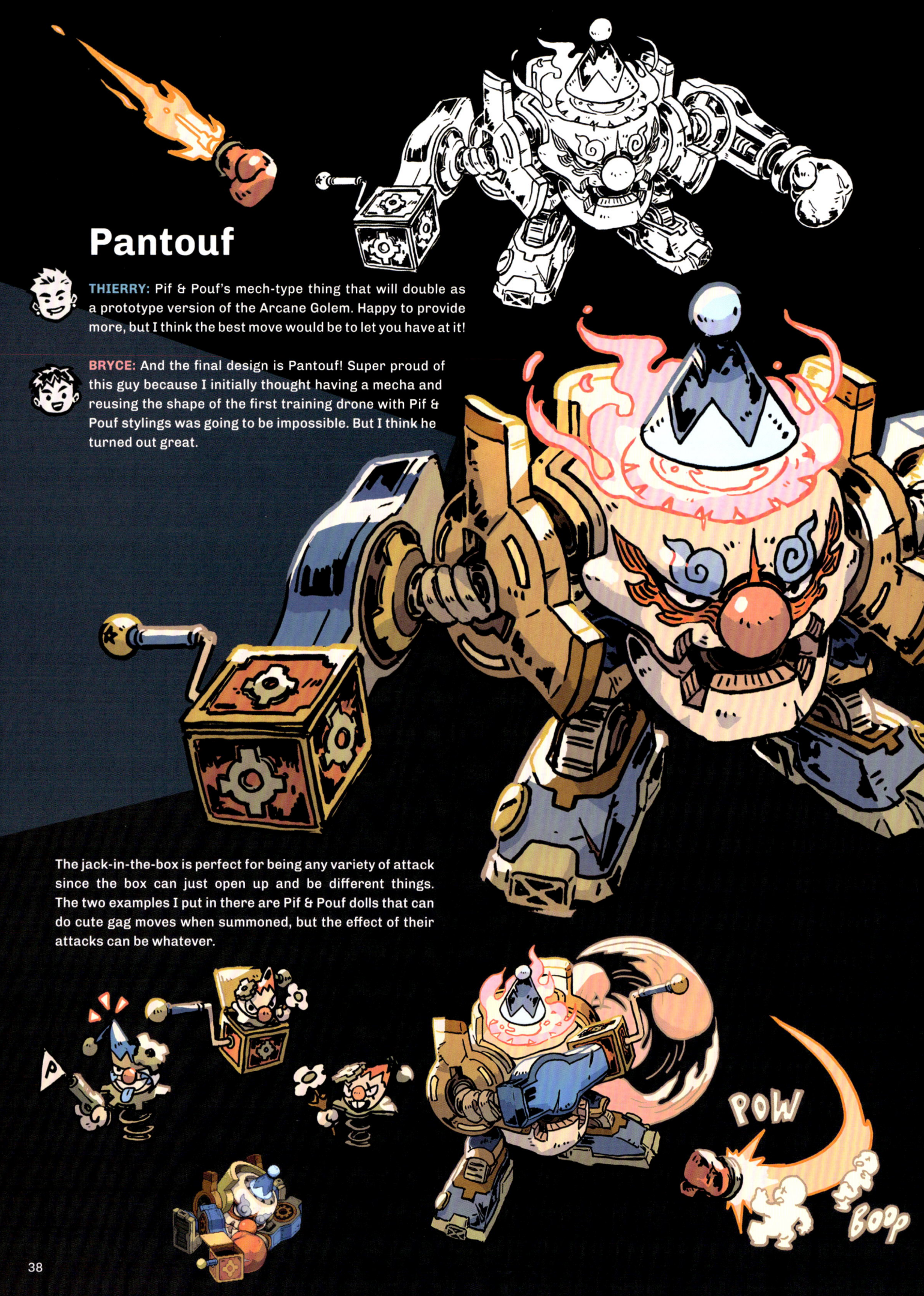

Pantouf

THIERRY: Pif & Pouf's mech-type thing that will double as a prototype version of the Arcane Golem. Happy to provide more, but I think the best move would be to let you have at it!

BRYCE: And the final design is Pantouf! Super proud of this guy because I initially thought having a mecha and reusing the shape of the first training drone with Pif & Pouf stylings was going to be impossible. But I think he turned out great.

The jack-in-the-box is perfect for being any variety of attack since the box can just open up and be different things. The two examples I put in there are Pif & Pouf dolls that can do cute gag moves when summoned, but the effect of their attacks can be whatever.

POW

BOOP

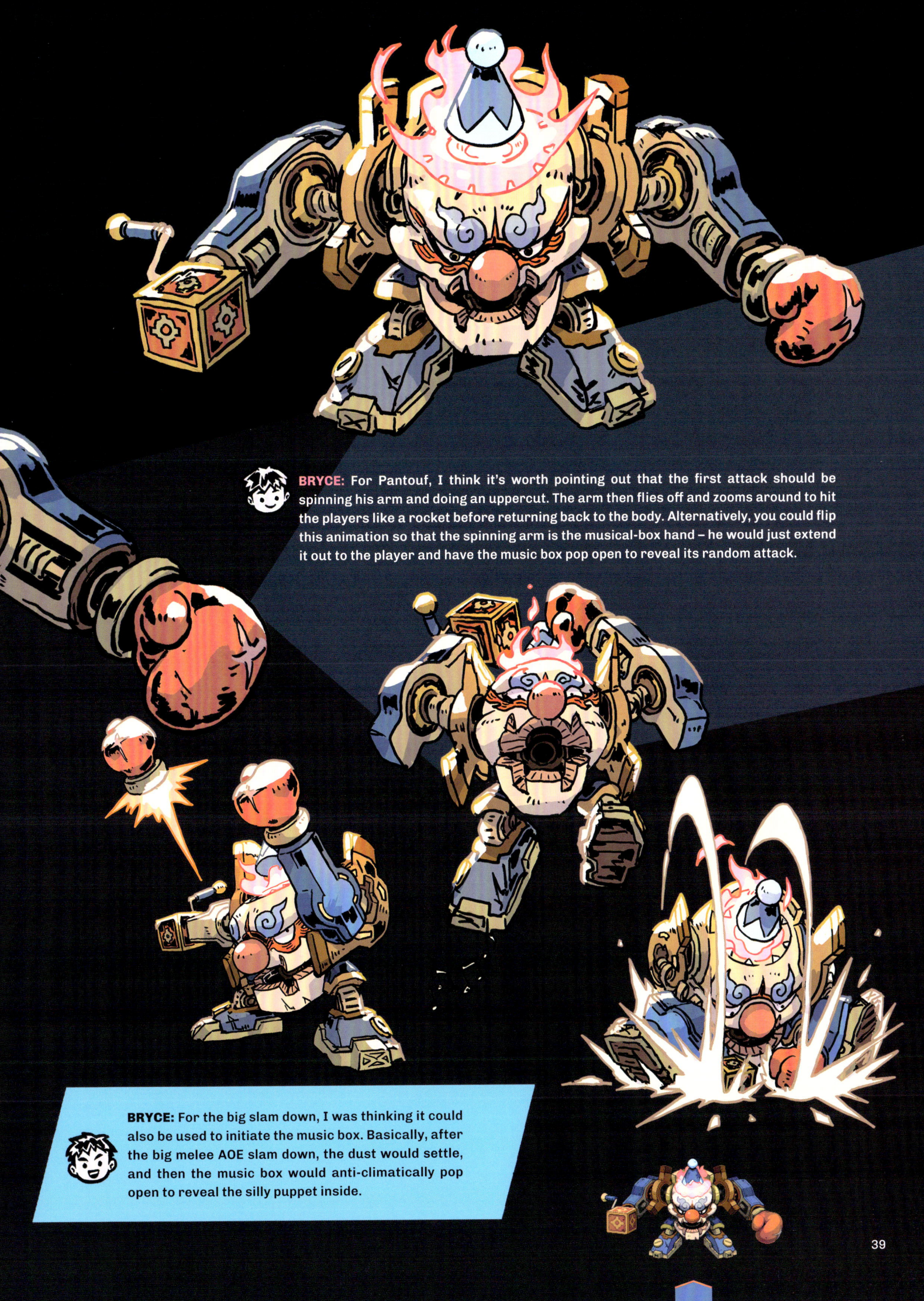

BRYCE: For Pantouf, I think it's worth pointing out that the first attack should be spinning his arm and doing an uppercut. The arm then flies off and zooms around to hit the players like a rocket before returning back to the body. Alternatively, you could flip this animation so that the spinning arm is the musical-box hand – he would just extend it out to the player and have the music box pop open to reveal its random attack.

BRYCE: For the big slam down, I was thinking it could also be used to initiate the music box. Basically, after the big melee AOE slam down, the dust would settle, and then the music box would anti-climatically pop open to reveal the silly puppet inside.

39

Evil Watchmaker

THIERRY: Aka, 'The Puppeteer'. She will appear as a giant arching over the scene, pulling the strings to put the Dweller together for the final fight. She sacrifices herself for it to come alive. If that image isn't clear, I still see the *King's Quest VII* key art here (kind of like Elysan'darëlle's final form). We also need the human-sized version; she'll transform into the giant puppeteer form to play the giant Wheels table, and then again later to activate the Dweller.

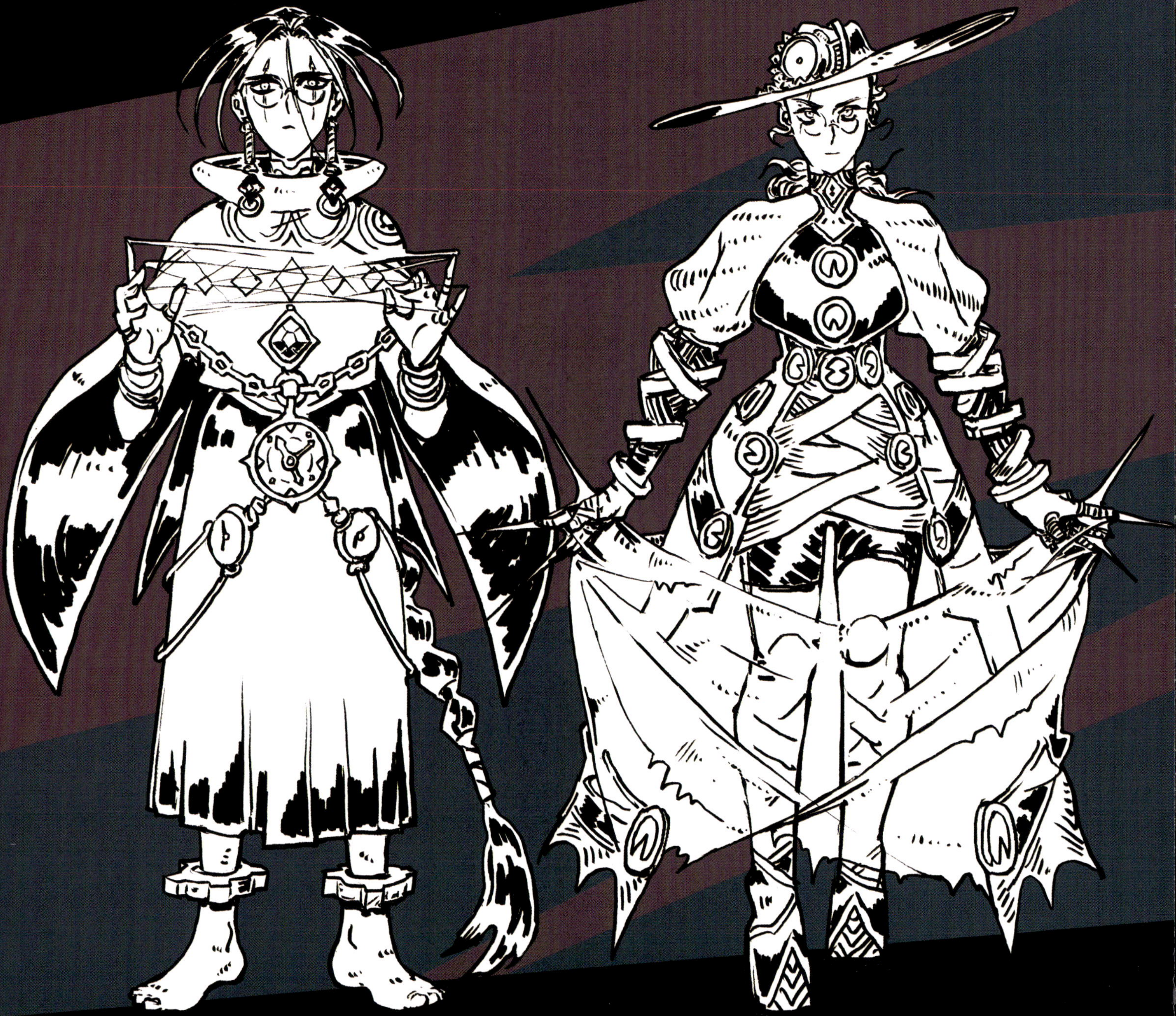

BRYCE: Fortune Teller Oracle – 90s after-school anime villain vibes (from *Sailor Moon* or *Hunter x Hunter*) with that bad hair (which I actually think is super fun). I love that she's the most puppeteer-esque, and that she's doing a sort of cats cradle to do her magic, which would be cool in a giant head/hands fight. I feel like I've tried using clockwork cogs for just about everything by this point except shackles. They have a creepy religious vibe, which is perfect for this cult priestess if she's going to kill herself to summon the Clockwork Dweller.

Dark Librarian – My first instinct on what an evil version of the Watchmaker would look like. Somehow still Victorian, intellectual, and fancy, but in a more gaudy and arrogant way, as if her obsession has pushed her too far in all aspects. I somehow viewed the puppet-master motif as web-like? It might be nonsense, but I followed that line of thinking by making her dress a part of that web and giving her some very lacy garments. I always felt the Watchermaker's vibe was a bit arrogant, but this lady is a straight up bitch, lol.

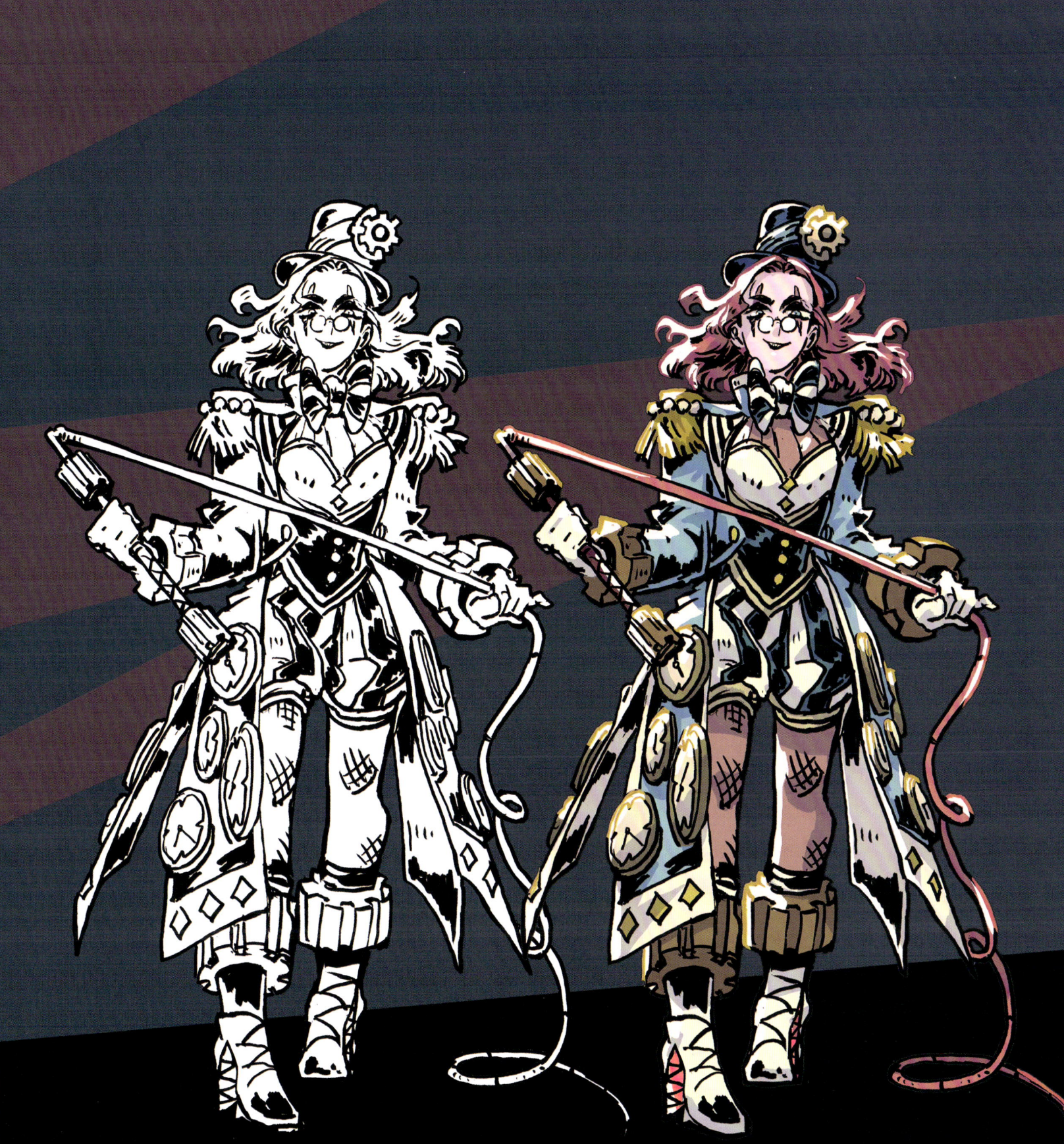

Ringmaster – Trying to follow the circus and clockwork theme to its most logical conclusion. I like that she fits that setting the most and has the strongest contrast from the original Watchmaker. Similar to Zale, it's almost like an inner vice of wanting attention/control has given birth to this whip-wielding version. I'm not sure how much dialogue would need tweaking to match the switch to a ringmaster versus a puppeteer, though. I think she might be cool enough to consider having her boss form whipping a giant minion around instead of a giant head/hand setup.

THIERRY: Well, in the spirit of respecting your presentation, I read through them all. But to be honest, it was Ringmaster right away. All great options as always, but this one is simply, purely 'it'. Open to discussion as always if you have any strong feelings, but OMG she's fire.

Having said all this, to be extra clear, the 'boss fight' with her is really an indirect one anyway. She'll just be playing Wheels; we're figurine-sized on a table that's her size, so we never attack her directly. We just win by killing all her figurines, one after another.

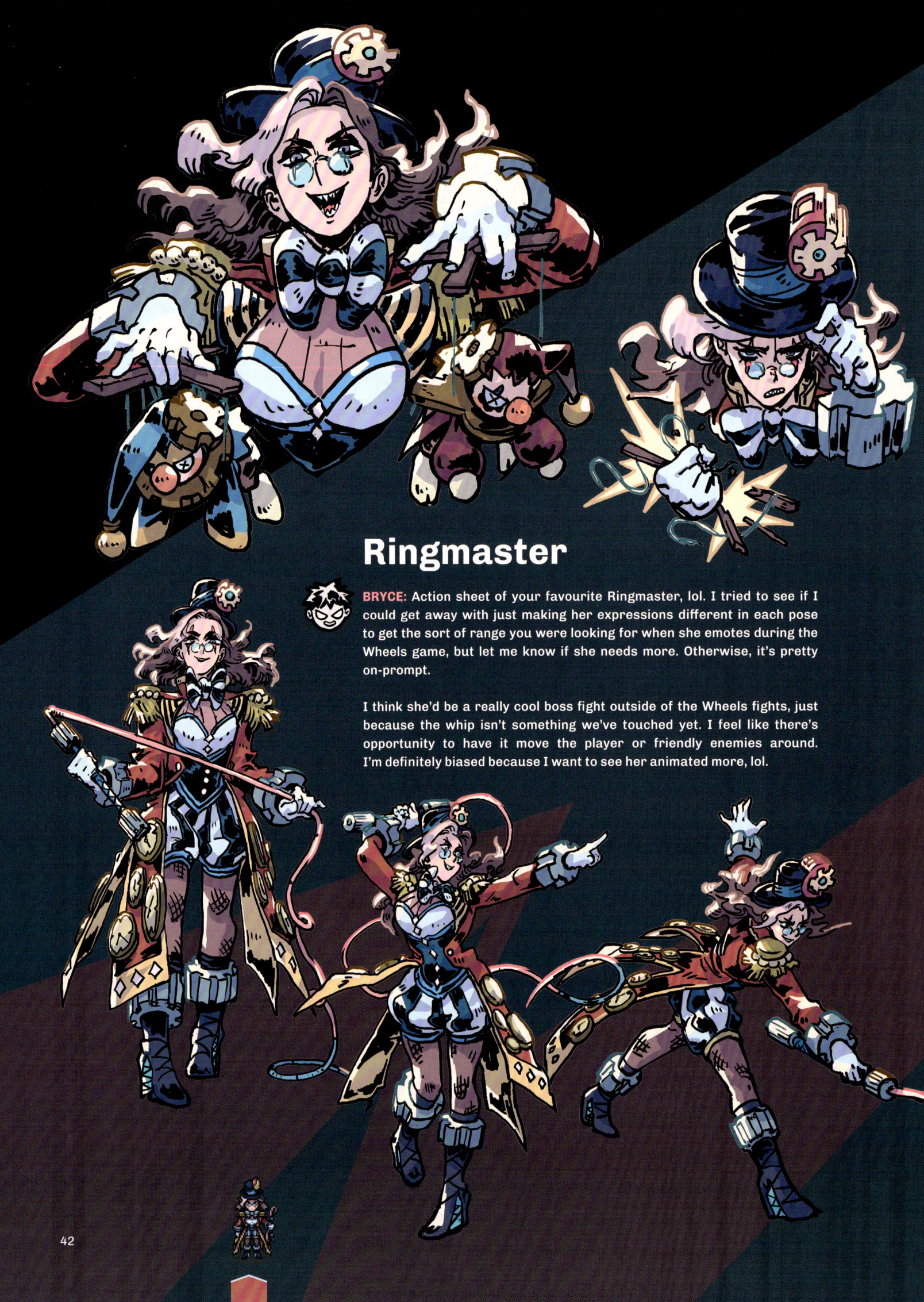

Ringmaster

BRYCE: Action sheet of your favourite Ringmaster, lol. I tried to see if I could get away with just making her expressions different in each pose to get the sort of range you were looking for when she emotes during the Wheels game, but let me know if she needs more. Otherwise, it's pretty on-prompt.

I think she'd be a really cool boss fight outside of the Wheels fights, just because the whip isn't something we've touched yet. I feel like there's opportunity to have it move the player or friendly enemies around. I'm definitely biased because I want to see her animated more, lol.

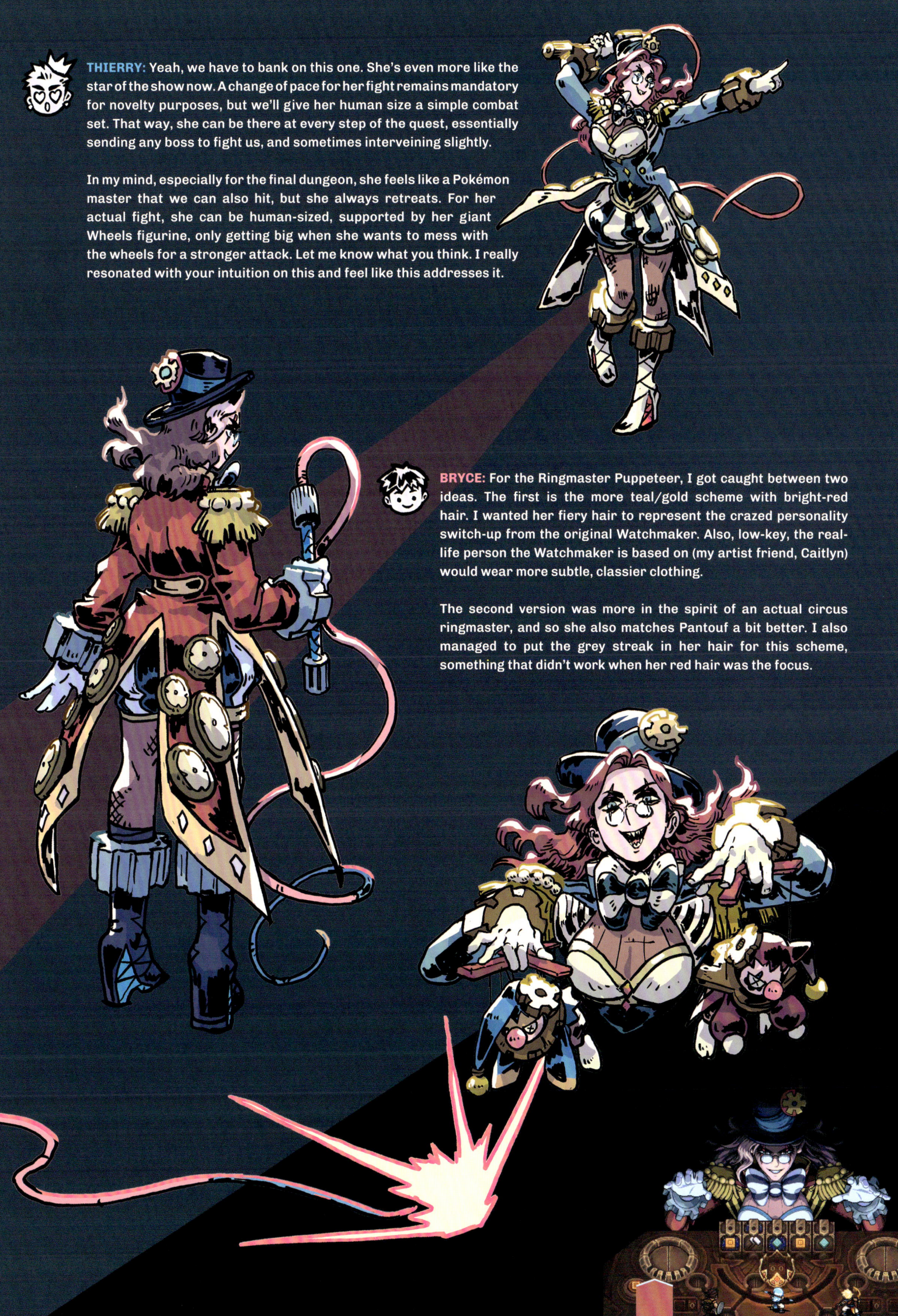

THIERRY: Yeah, we have to bank on this one. She's even more like the star of the show now. A change of pace for her fight remains mandatory for novelty purposes, but we'll give her human size a simple combat set. That way, she can be there at every step of the quest, essentially sending any boss to fight us, and sometimes intervening slightly.

In my mind, especially for the final dungeon, she feels like a Pokémon master that we can also hit, but she always retreats. For her actual fight, she can be human-sized, supported by her giant Wheels figurine, only getting big when she wants to mess with the wheels for a stronger attack. Let me know what you think. I really resonated with your intuition on this and feel like this addresses it.

BRYCE: For the Ringmaster Puppeteer, I got caught between two ideas. The first is the more teal/gold scheme with bright-red hair. I wanted her fiery hair to represent the crazed personality switch-up from the original Watchmaker. Also, low-key, the real-life person the Watchmaker is based on (my artist friend, Caitlyn) would wear more subtle, classier clothing.

The second version was more in the spirit of an actual circus ringmaster, and so she also matches Pantouf a bit better. I also managed to put the grey streak in her hair for this scheme, something that didn't work when her red hair was the focus.

Clockwork Dweller

THIERRY: Well, all the information is in the name for this one. However, in opening this up, I found a note I had left for my future-self explaining an option you made for the World Eater that I thought could be a pretty cool clockwork Dweller. It's this guy, who also seems to have a pet dragon of sorts. I remember feeling it could be a good fit if we did cogs rather than bones.

BRYCE: Followed your prompt on reusing the design originally meant for the World Eater! Only thing worth noting is that my first pass at this had a lot more unique cog shapes, but I felt like it would be hell for the animators. So, I swapped out a lot of the pieces to reuse the same circular-cog shape. It still might be hell for the animators, but hopefully they can reuse a lot of the same pieces.

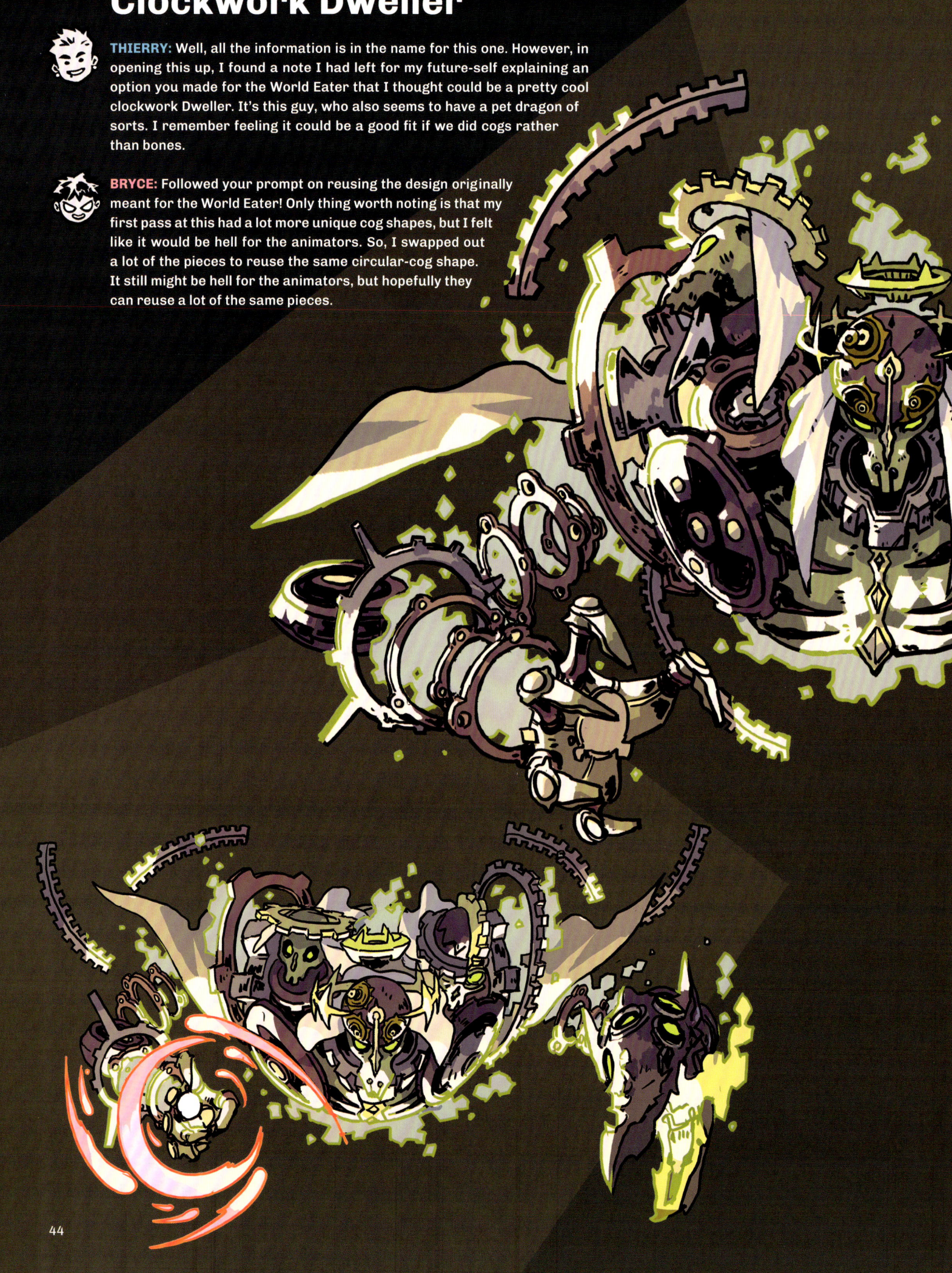

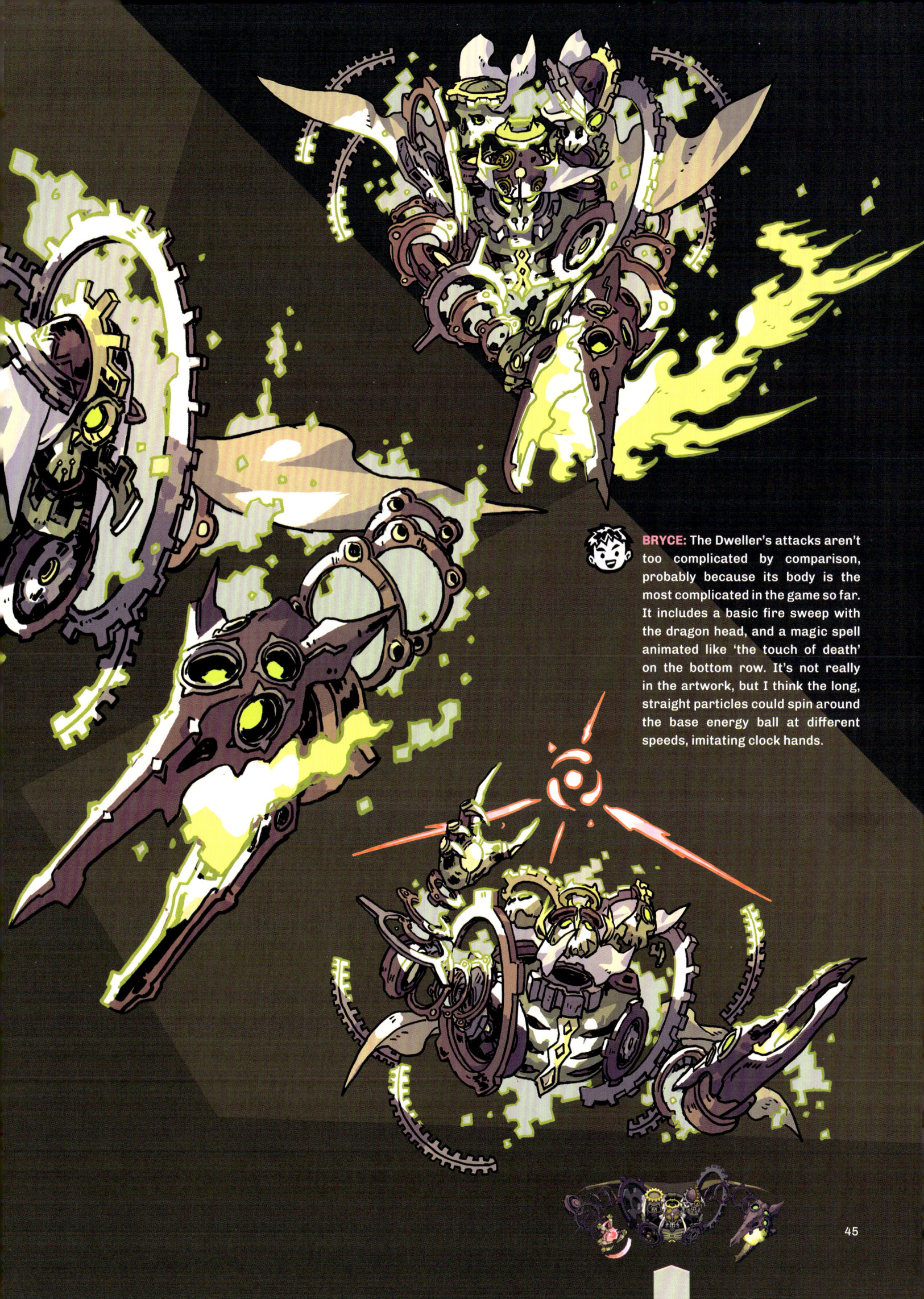

BRYCE: The Dweller's attacks aren't too complicated by comparison, probably because its body is the most complicated in the game so far. It includes a basic fire sweep with the dragon head, and a magic spell animated like 'the touch of death' on the bottom row. It's not really in the artwork, but I think the long, straight particles could spin around the base energy ball at different speeds, imitating clock hands.

Gator Spearman

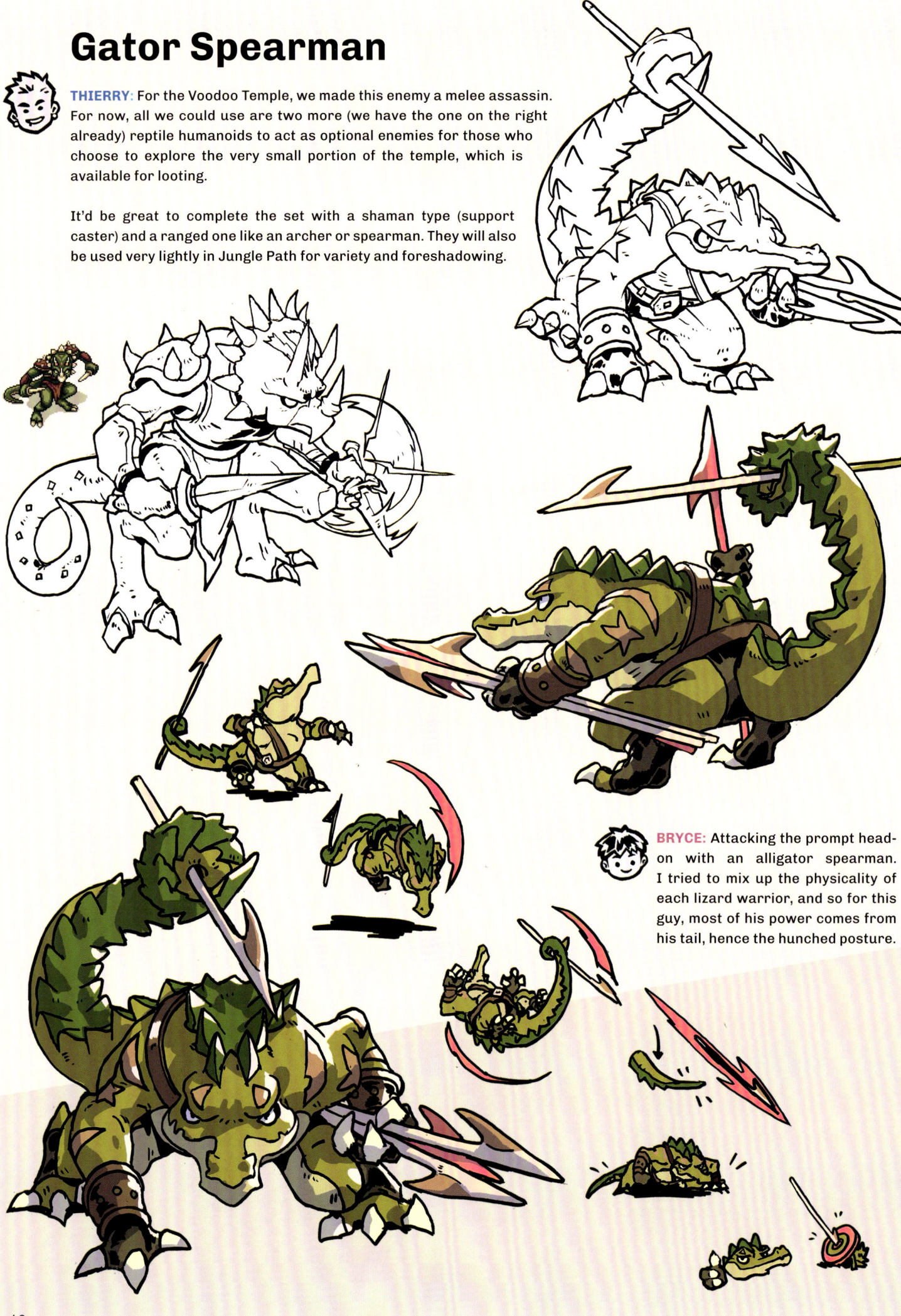

THIERRY: For the Voodoo Temple, we made this enemy a melee assassin. For now, all we could use are two more (we have the one on the right already) reptile humanoids to act as optional enemies for those who choose to explore the very small portion of the temple, which is available for looting.

It'd be great to complete the set with a shaman type (support caster) and a ranged one like an archer or spearman. They will also be used very lightly in Jungle Path for variety and foreshadowing.

BRYCE: Attacking the prompt head-on with an alligator spearman. I tried to mix up the physicality of each lizard warrior, and so for this guy, most of his power comes from his tail, hence the hunched posture.

Rattler Shaman

PRESENT-DAY BRYCE: A couple things that changed from the initial concept to the coloured version are the tail and the staff. While trying to think of attacks for a shaman, I came up with the idea of him having a powerful fire-breathing attack – this required changing the normal shaman staff into a torch and giving him something to do while waiting a turn to attack, hence the rattler tail.

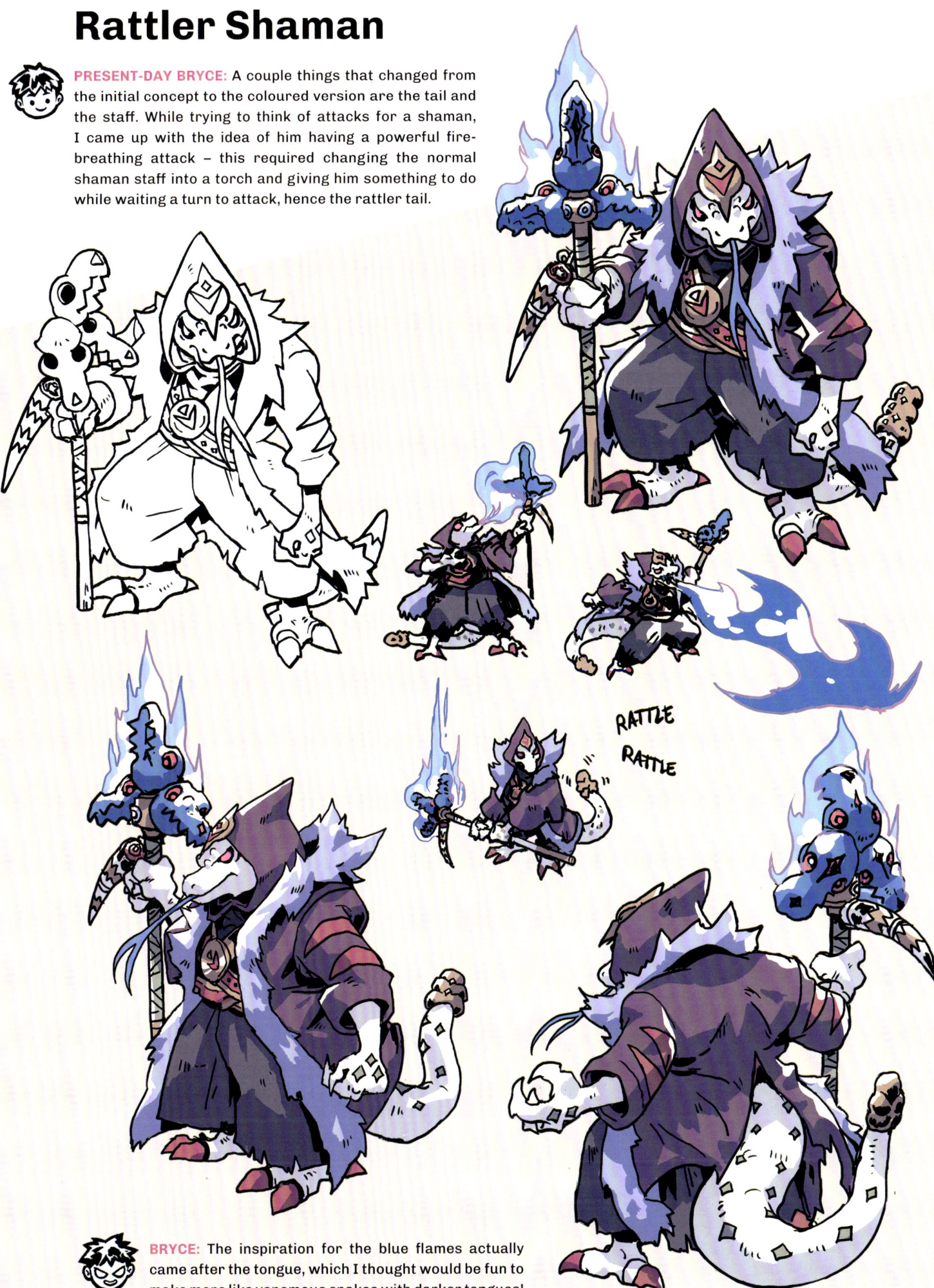

RATTLE
RATTLE

BRYCE: The inspiration for the blue flames actually came after the tongue, which I thought would be fun to make more like venomous snakes with darker tongues!

47

Chameleon Mage

BRYCE: The support caster you asked for! Admittedly, the main thing I was interested in exploring with this guy was using his tail as a third arm for holding his spellbook in an orchestra conductor sort of way.

I think it's fun if you can see what's inside his spellbook when he's facing away from the camera. For this to work, however, the contents of the book would need to be very simple (basically just a symbol per page). The fun easter egg would be that he then casts spells that use said symbol.

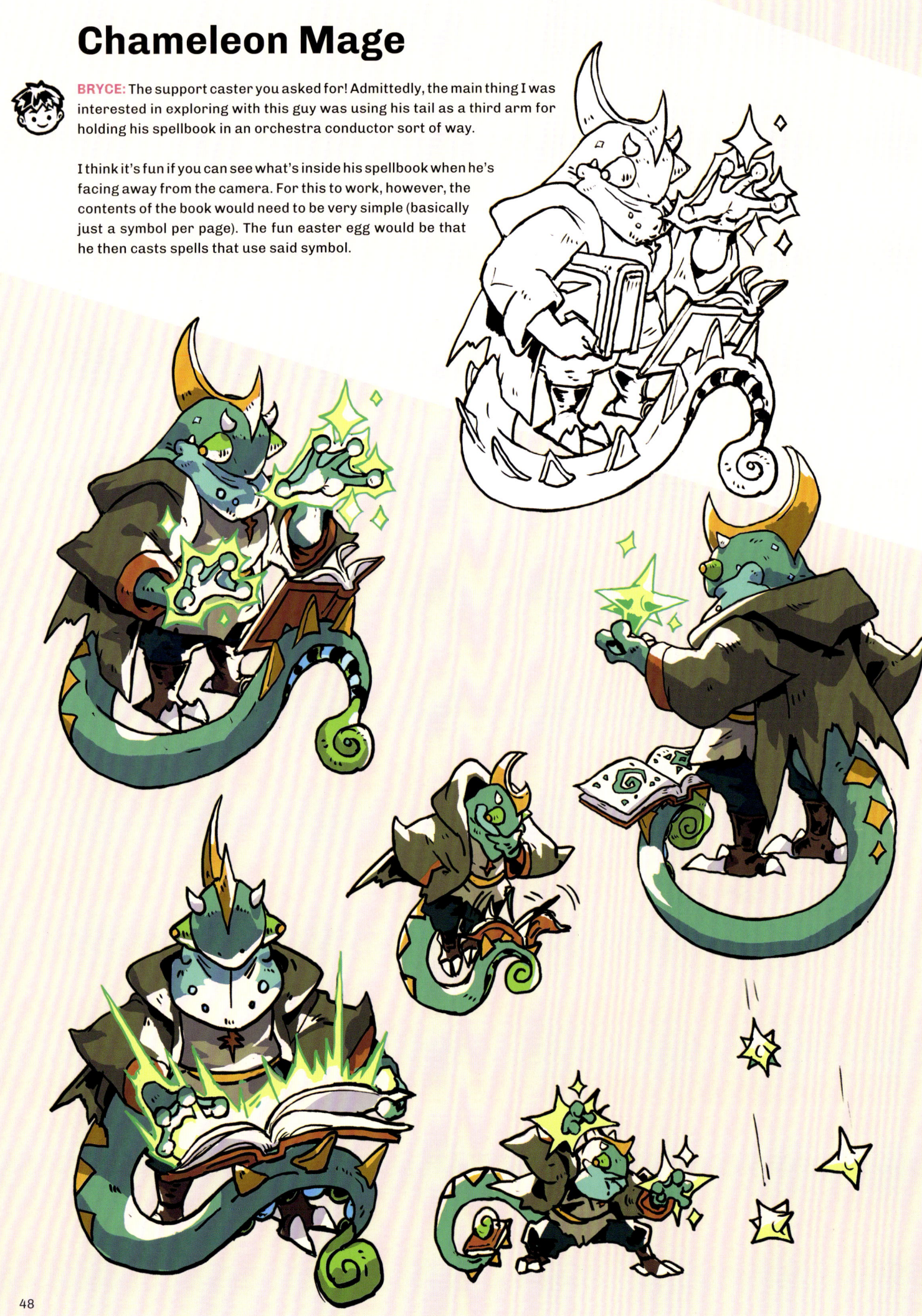

Rep Rider

PRESENT-DAY BRYCE: As usual, doing my extra silly take on the final option. What's a sillier reptile enemy than a reptile who rides another reptile?

After getting approval from Thierry, the biggest changes were to differentiate the Rider from the Gator Spearman, since we couldn't have the overlap with the same weapon choice.

With that in mind, I wanted to find a way to use this weapon change to create a more cohesive design with the mount. After deciding on the axe, I worked the same shape into the mount's snout and tail.

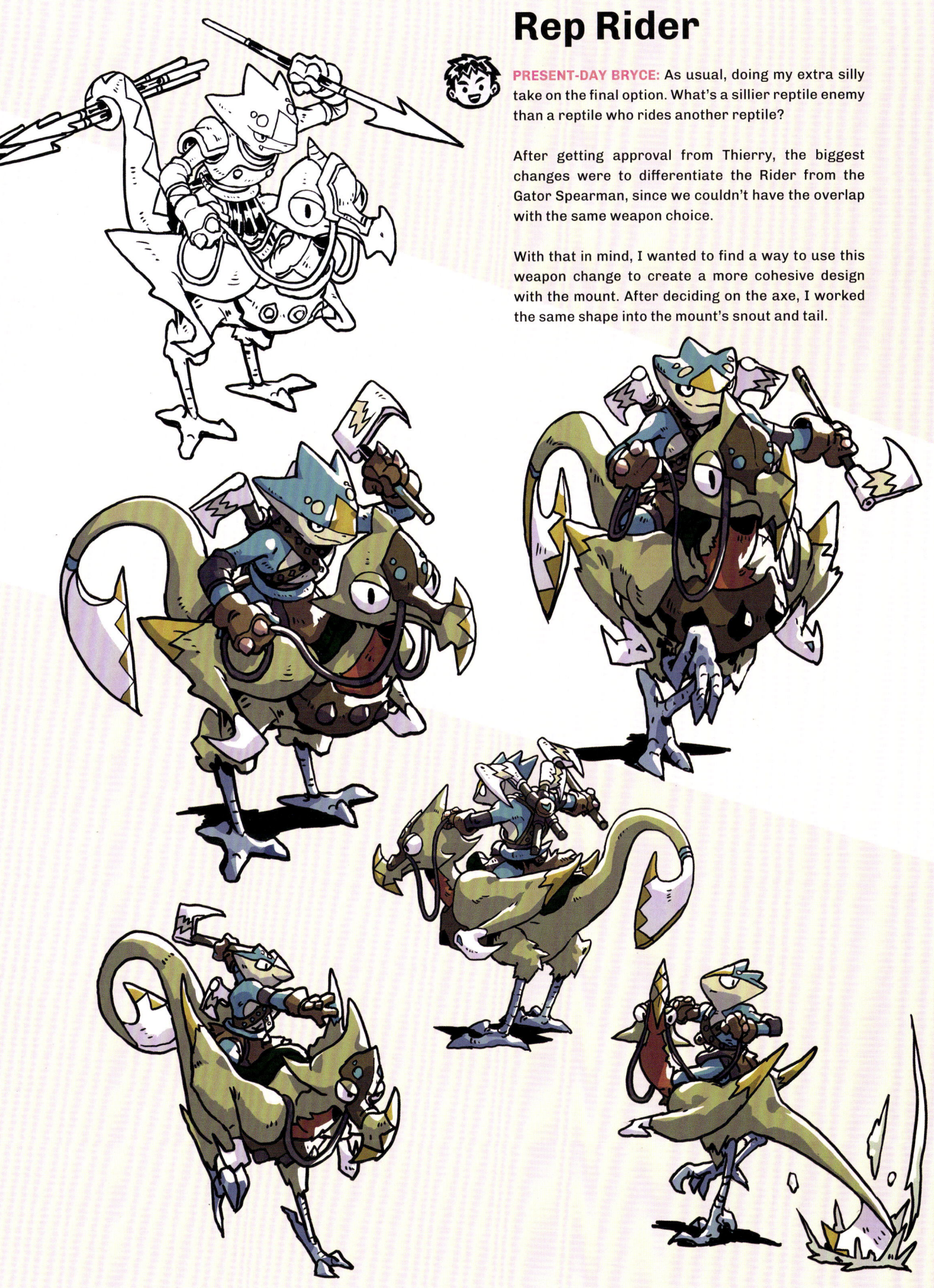

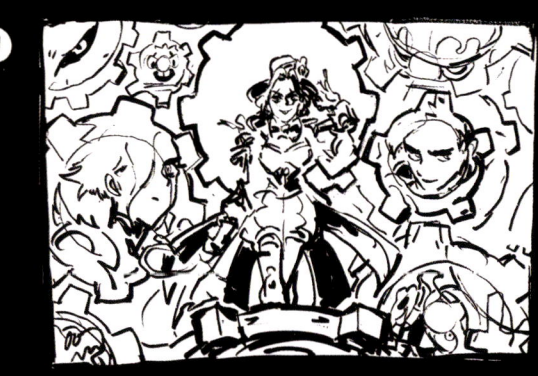

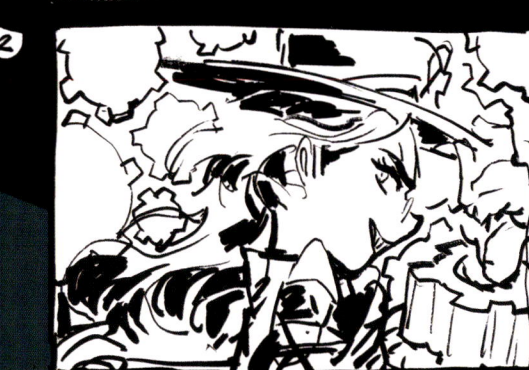

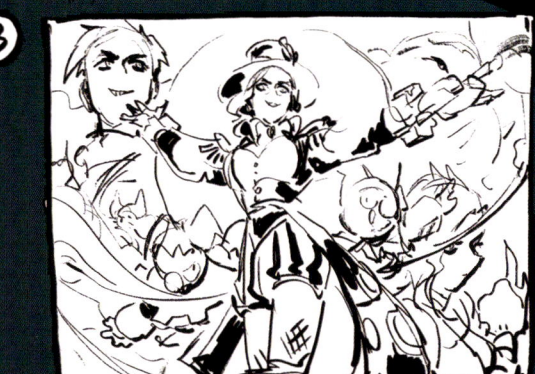

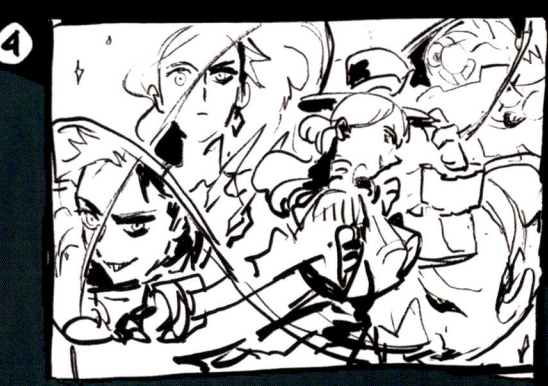

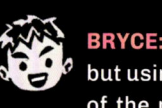

BRYCE: 1. Cog Moon – First idea is to mirror the original key art but using elements of the Watchmaker's environment (cogs in place of the moon and foreground). Note that the cog shape is actually the negative space of a bunch of other clock machinery, and so she's actually backlit as well. Then to add the other characters, I'd superimpose them on the cogs, almost like windows into the alternate universe.

2. Watchmaker's Cog Design – Matching more closely to the idea you pitched where we can get much closer to the Watchmaker and then use cog shapes to house all the other characters behind her. A bigger change-up to get such a tight close-up.

3. Grand Circus – Similar idea to #1 but with a spotlight on the Watchmaker to mirror the moon. The clown duo also poses next to her to emphasize this theme and we rely on the cogs on their outfits to get across the clockwork motifs of the DLC. In the shadows, you'll find close-up shots of the other characters we want to highlight.

4. Whip Dimension – A wider shot of the Watchmaker in action and where the background elements are spaced out by her whip. My favourite detail here is normal Valere and Zale on one side of the whip and then their evil counterparts on the other.

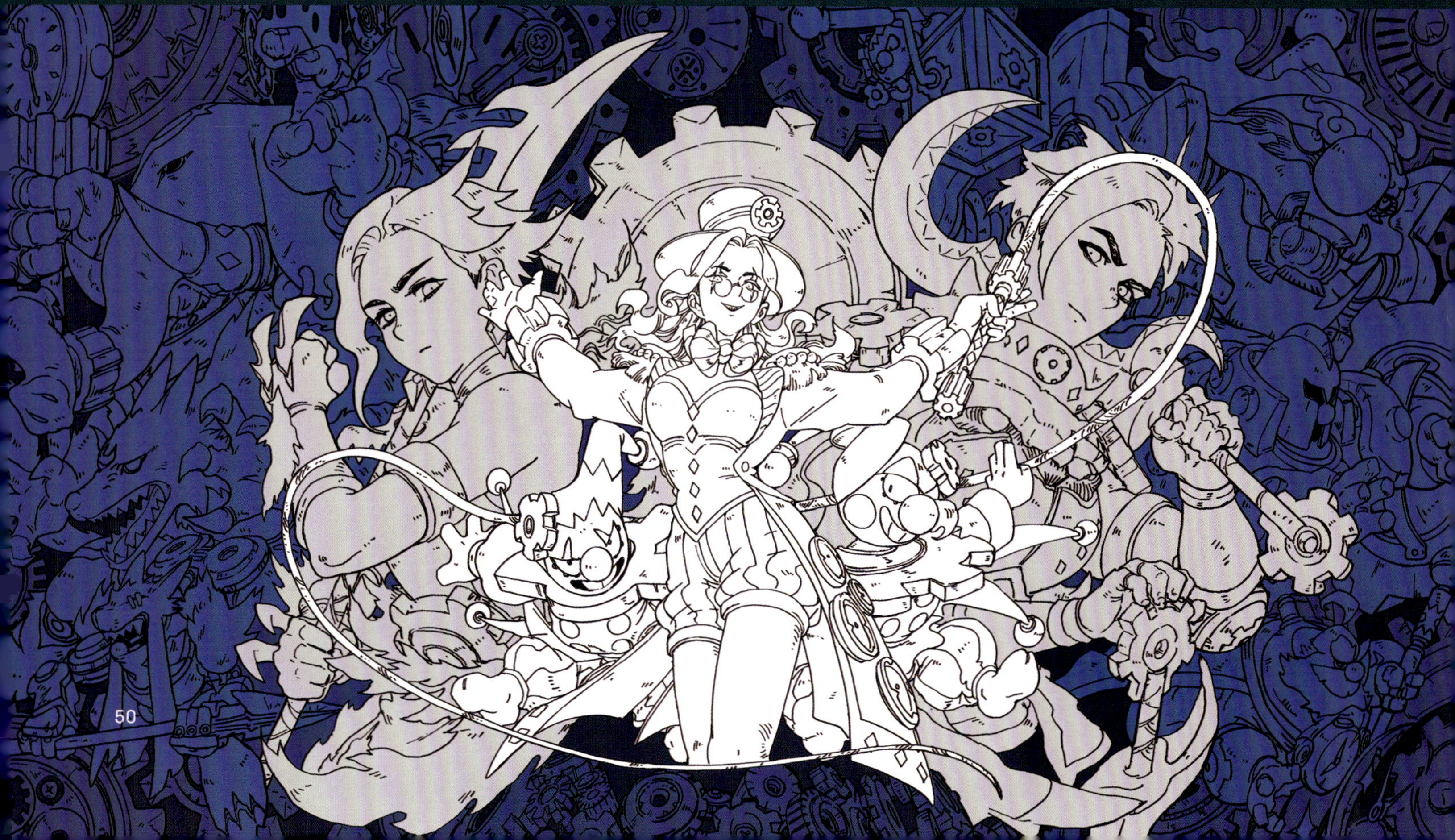

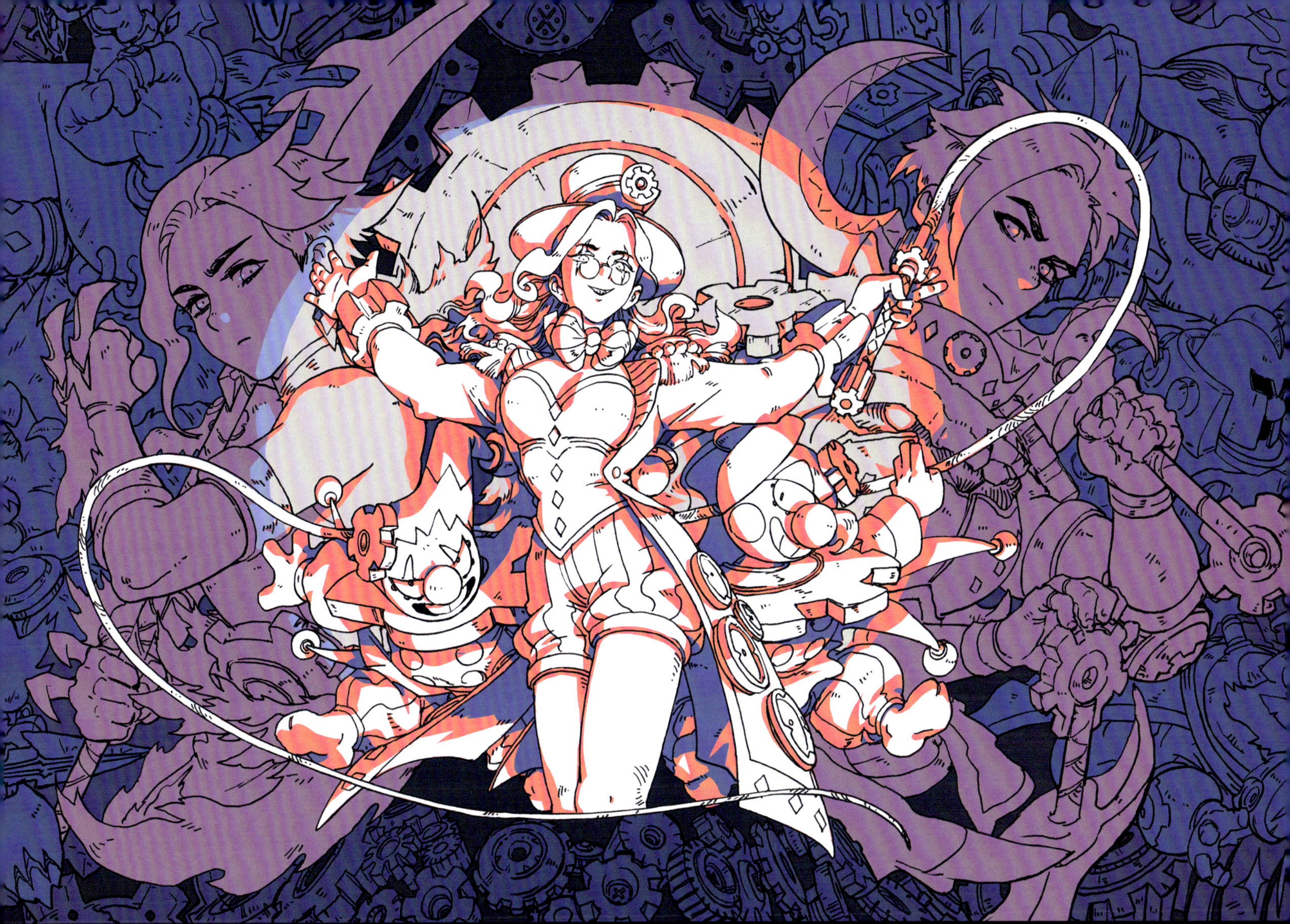

BRYCE: Oh hey, I also forgot to send you WIPs of the key art. This is just the line art with the sections masked off. And this is with the spotlight effect. I'm planning to do a sort of offset spotlight where the two light sources are blue and red, which will also splash onto Valere and Zale to match their sun/moon affinities.

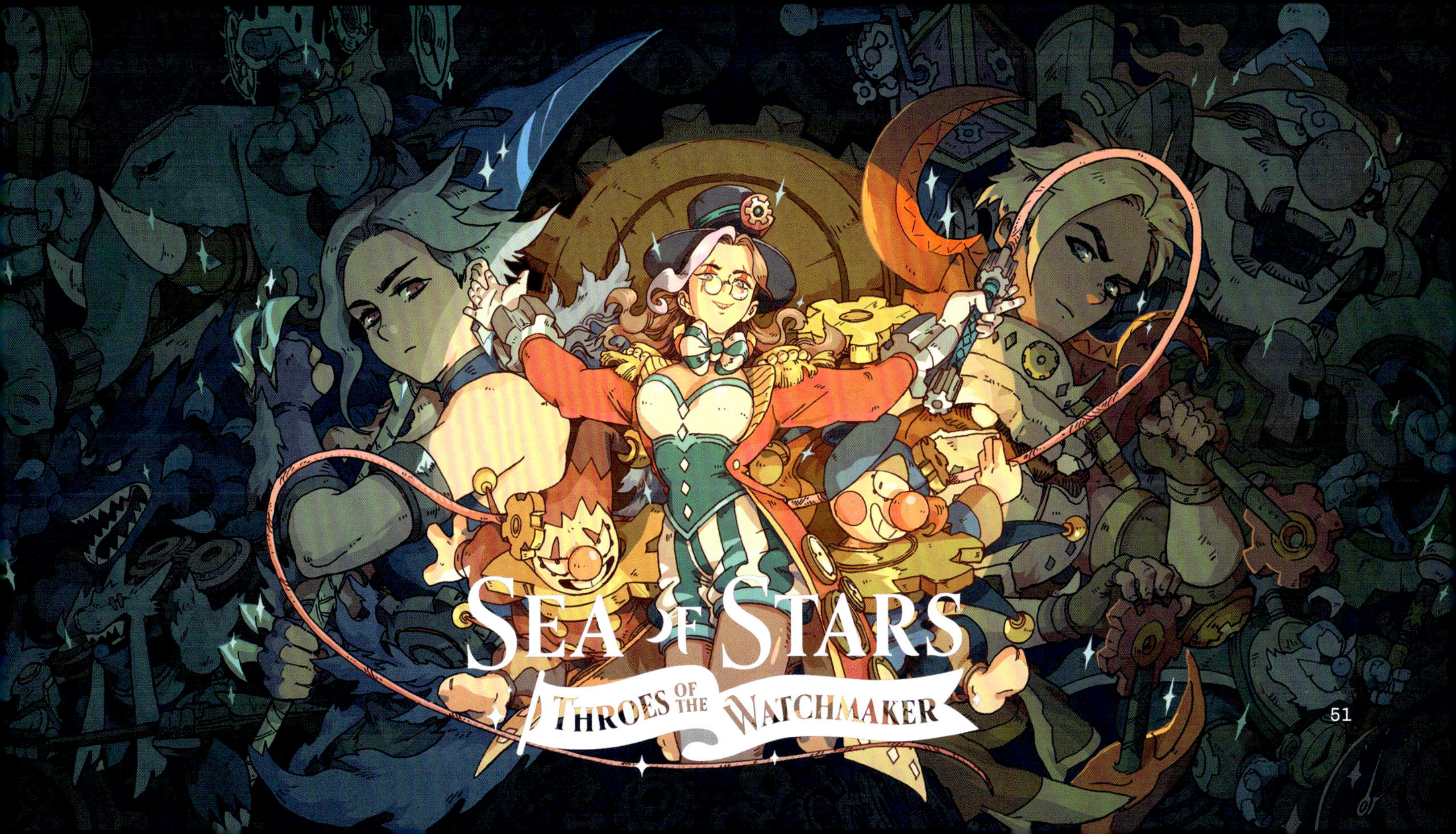

SEA OF STARS
THROES OF THE WATCHMAKER

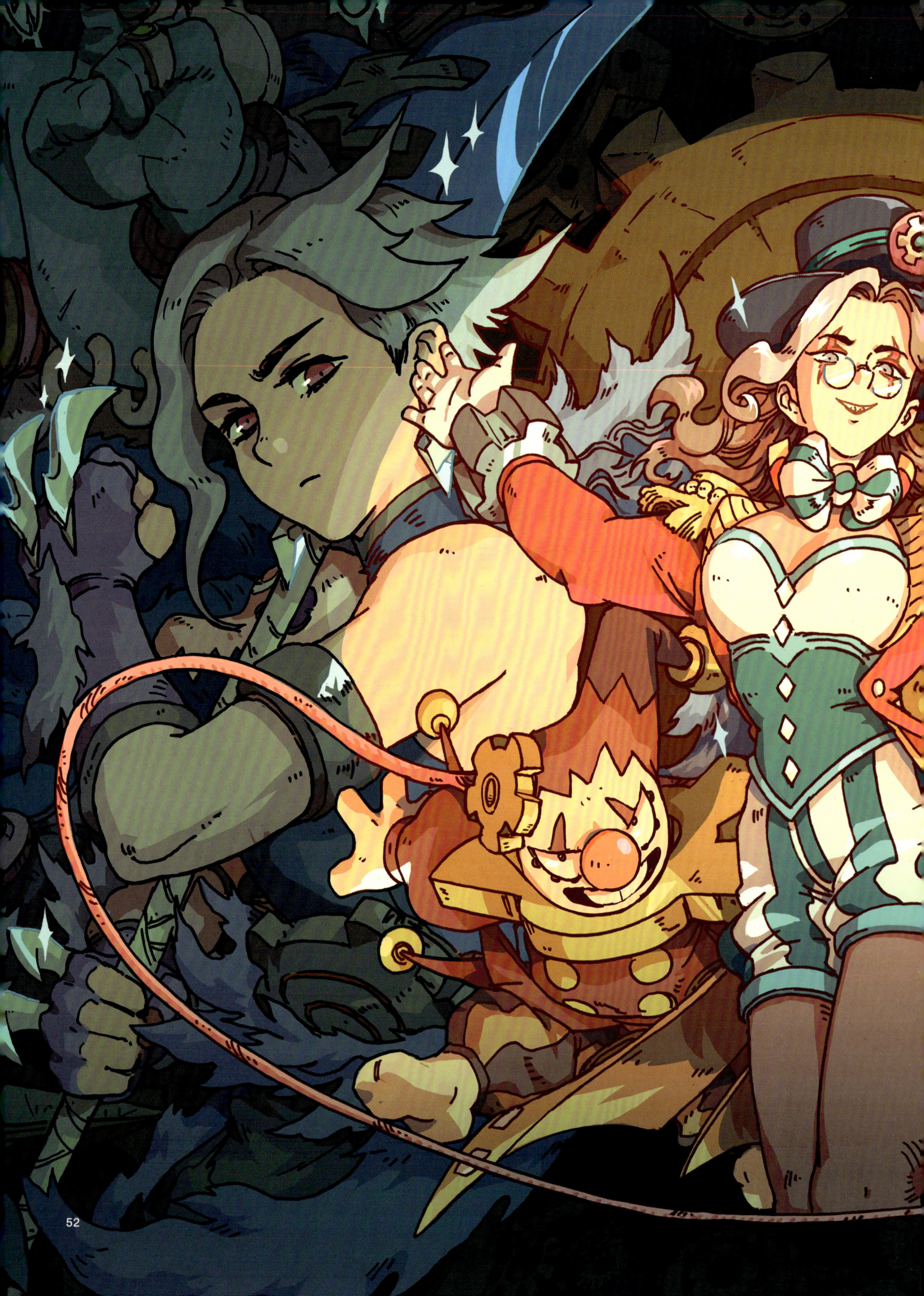

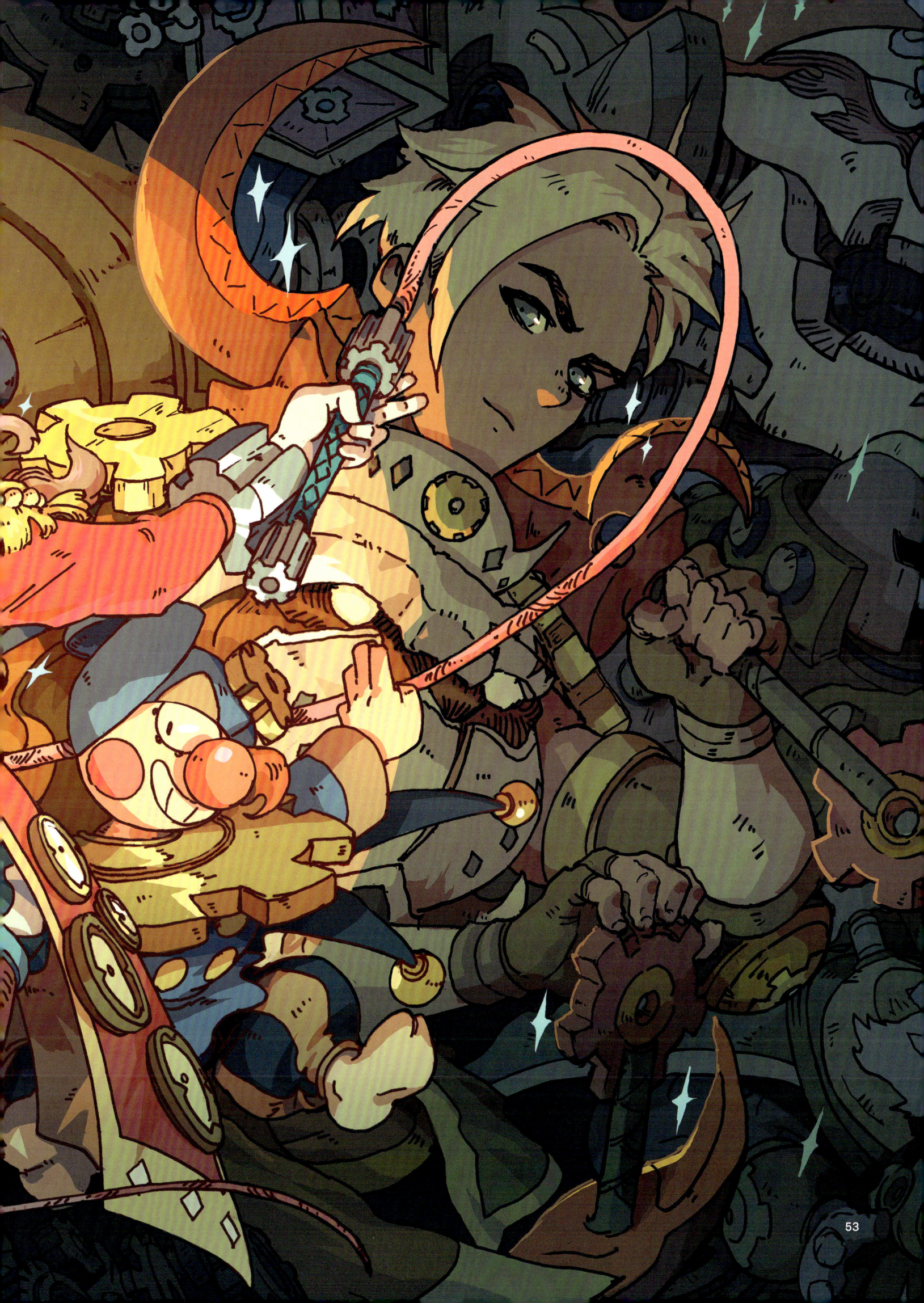

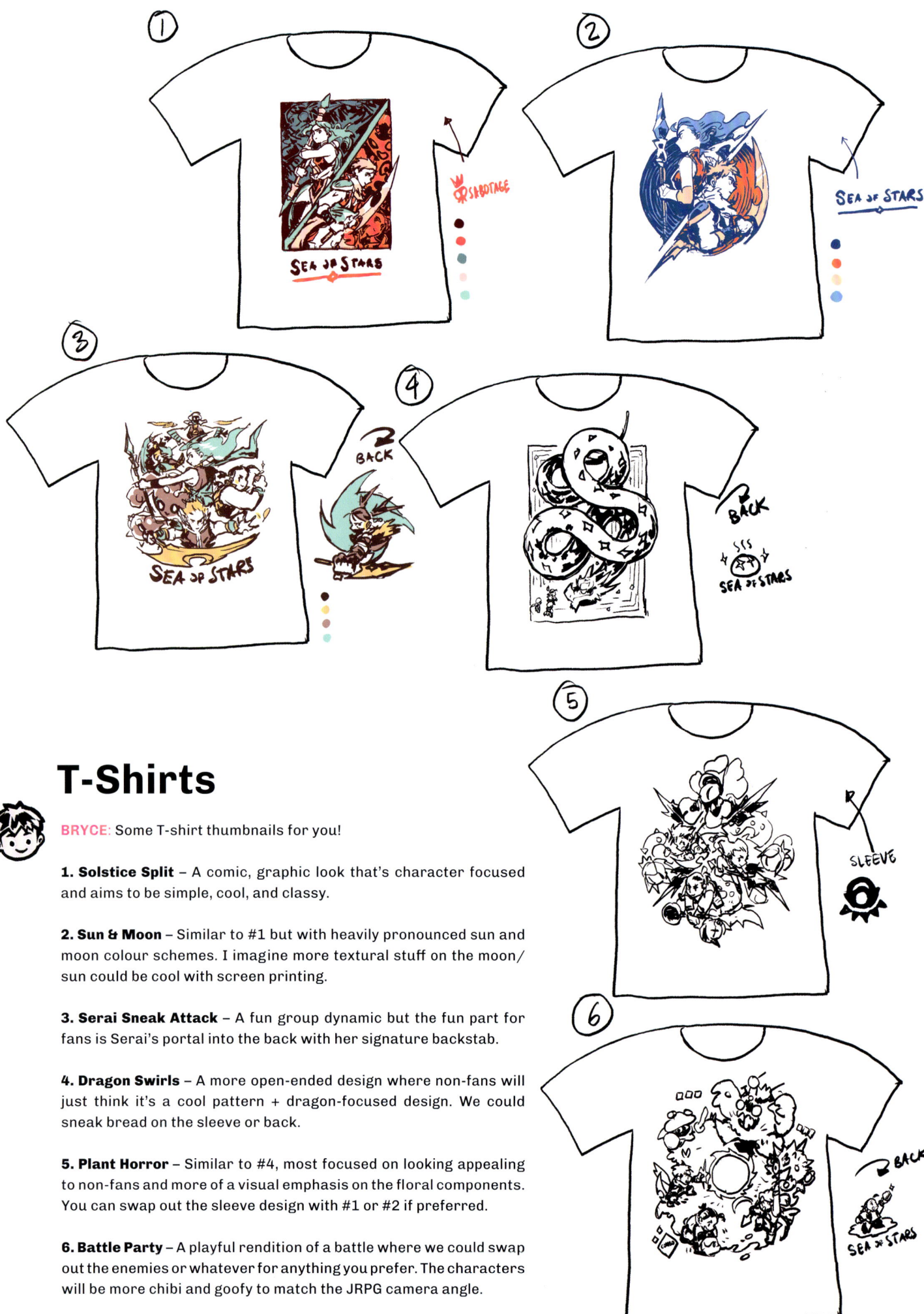

T-Shirts

BRYCE: Some T-shirt thumbnails for you!

1. Solstice Split – A comic, graphic look that's character focused and aims to be simple, cool, and classy.

2. Sun & Moon – Similar to #1 but with heavily pronounced sun and moon colour schemes. I imagine more textural stuff on the moon/sun could be cool with screen printing.

3. Serai Sneak Attack – A fun group dynamic but the fun part for fans is Serai's portal into the back with her signature backstab.

4. Dragon Swirls – A more open-ended design where non-fans will just think it's a cool pattern + dragon-focused design. We could sneak bread on the sleeve or back.

5. Plant Horror – Similar to #4, most focused on looking appealing to non-fans and more of a visual emphasis on the floral components. You can swap out the sleeve design with #1 or #2 if preferred.

6. Battle Party – A playful rendition of a battle where we could swap out the enemies or whatever for anything you prefer. The characters will be more chibi and goofy to match the JRPG camera angle.

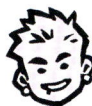 **THIERRY:** I'll go unfiltered on each, with the note that I think you should have the final say on this special piece.

Solstice Split – Good solid 'basic done right'. I think this is what people will expect (in a good way).

Sun & Moon – I'm not visualizing the difference very well I think, but just as a product, I feel it has the same potential and value as #1, so it would be down to which of the two you feel more strongly about.

Serai Sneak Attack – I think I'd go for this one since we rarely had official pieces with more characters.

Dragon Swirls – I would say this one is probably not recognizable enough. It would be great as an option if we were also doing a 'nail on the head/basic done right' shirt, but I don't think it's on the nose enough to be the only one.

Plant Horror – I like it, but I'd say it's the one easy pass since we had the botanical horror on a magazine cover already.

Battle Party – Gut feeling my favourite one conceptually, but marketing and recognition-wise might not scratch the proper itch (as a print though?).

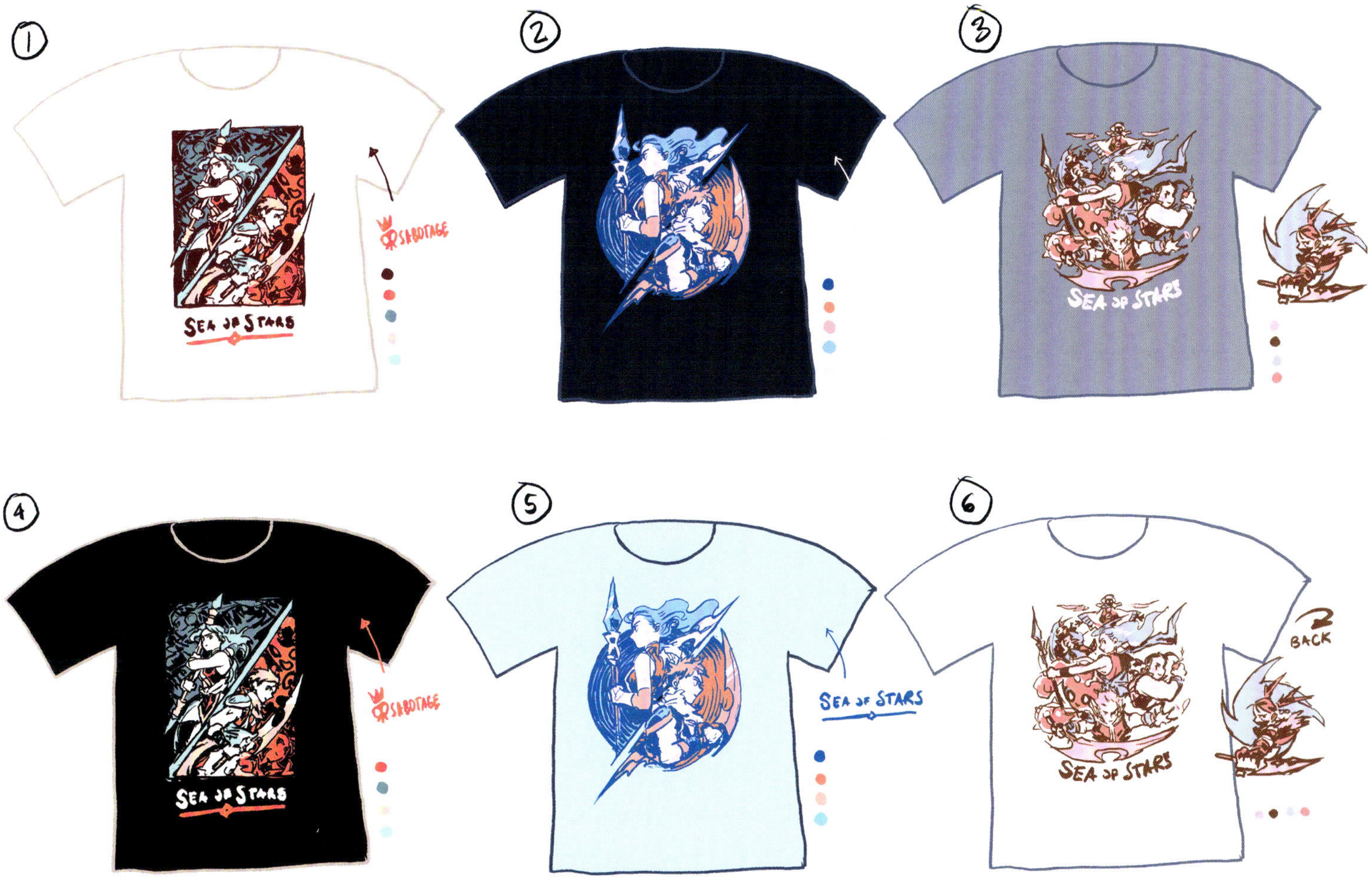

 BRYCE: Coloured thumbnails to give you a clearer picture of what I'm thinking with each design. I think it's pretty self-explanatory, except that I'd like to point out that the colours and shirt colours are super flexible, so try not to let that part of the design skew your decision.

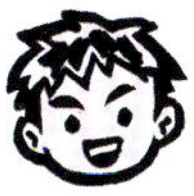

I guess this is why I don't normally do coloured thumbnails because it's so much more time-consuming and can be misleading, lol.

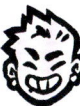 **THIERRY:** Gut reaction here is #1 and #4 catch my eye the most with the contrast, and #3 and #6 are my theoretical faves.

The latter, then? I think since we follow our gut feelings on the first pass, and they're all within the 'safe ones' category.

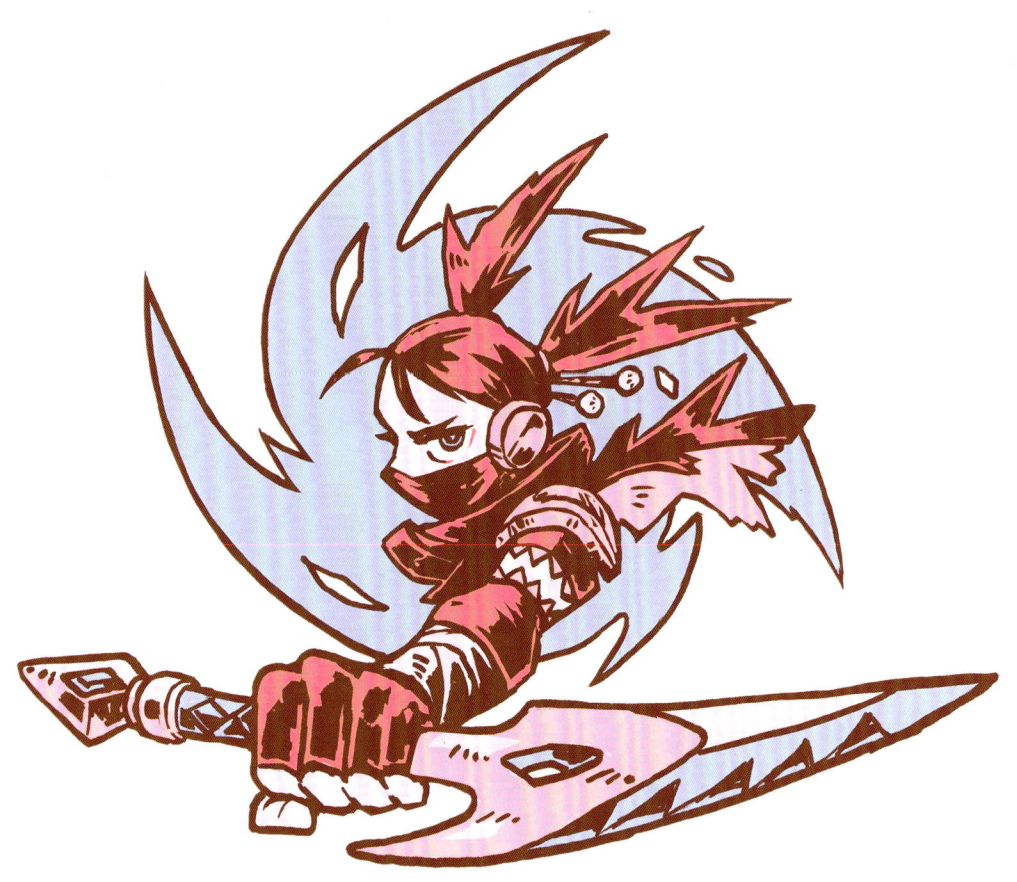

SEA OF STARS: *Solstice Warriors - Tee Shirt - by Sabotage*

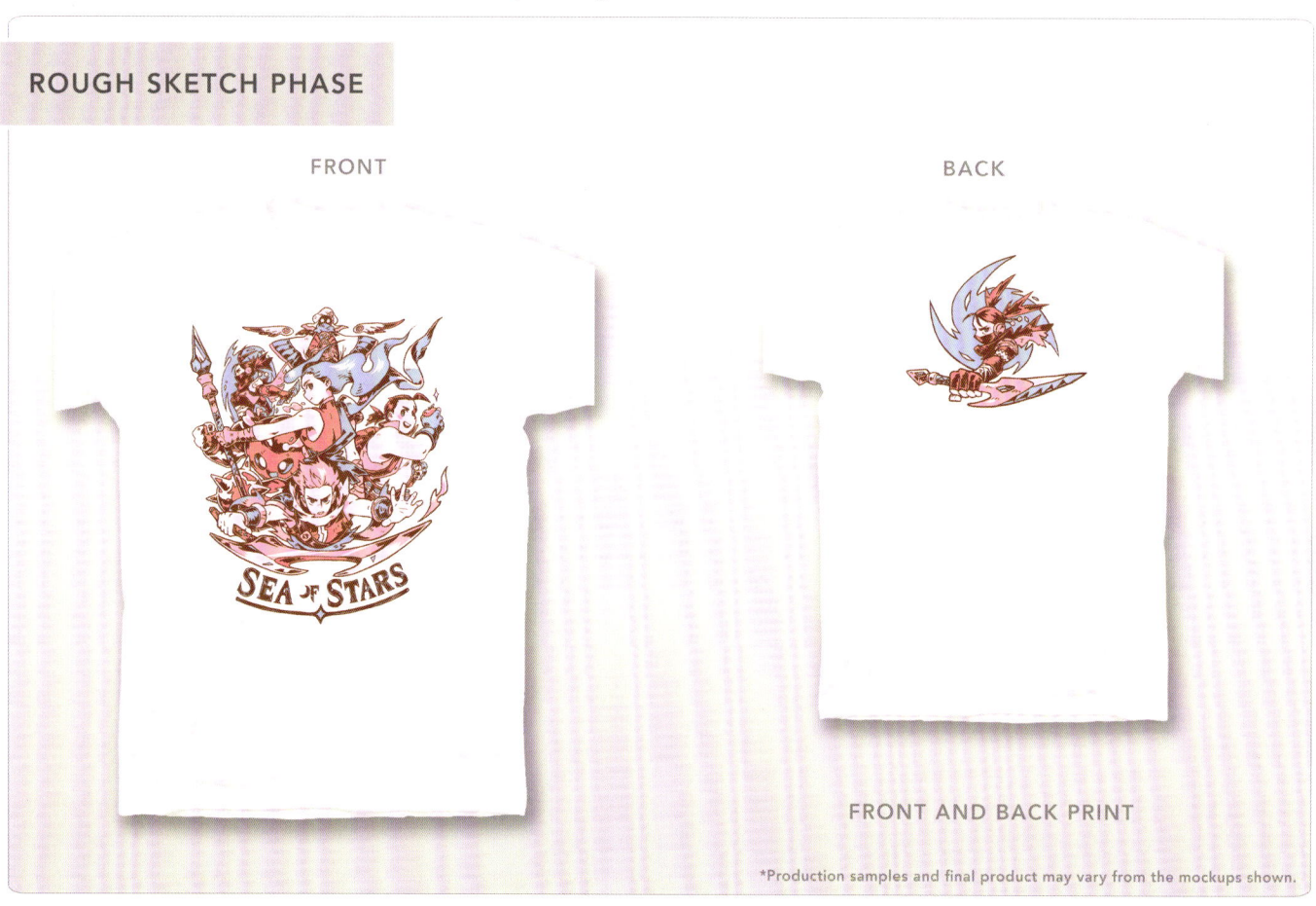

ROUGH SKETCH PHASE

FRONT

BACK

FRONT AND BACK PRINT

*Production samples and final product may vary from the mockups shown.

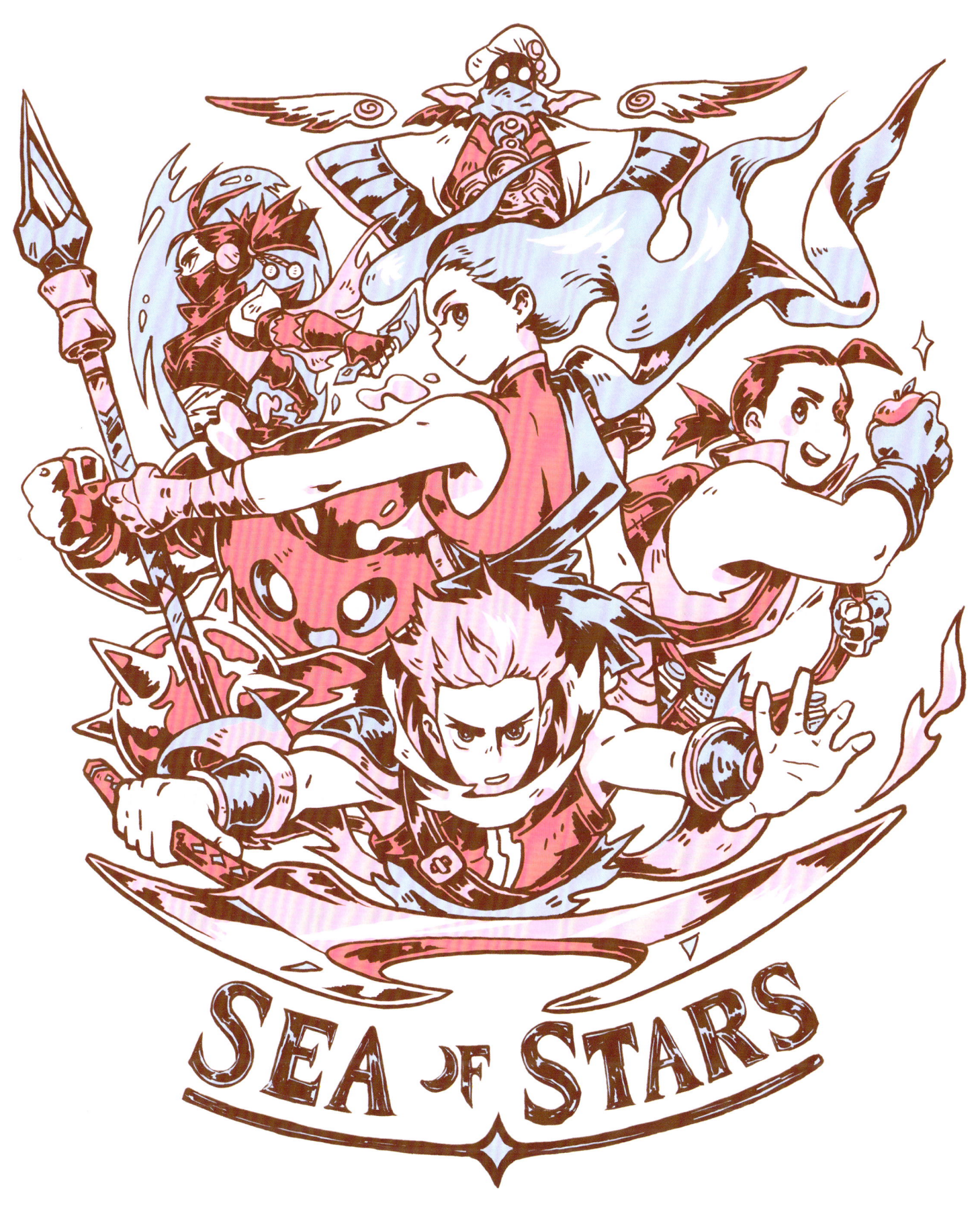

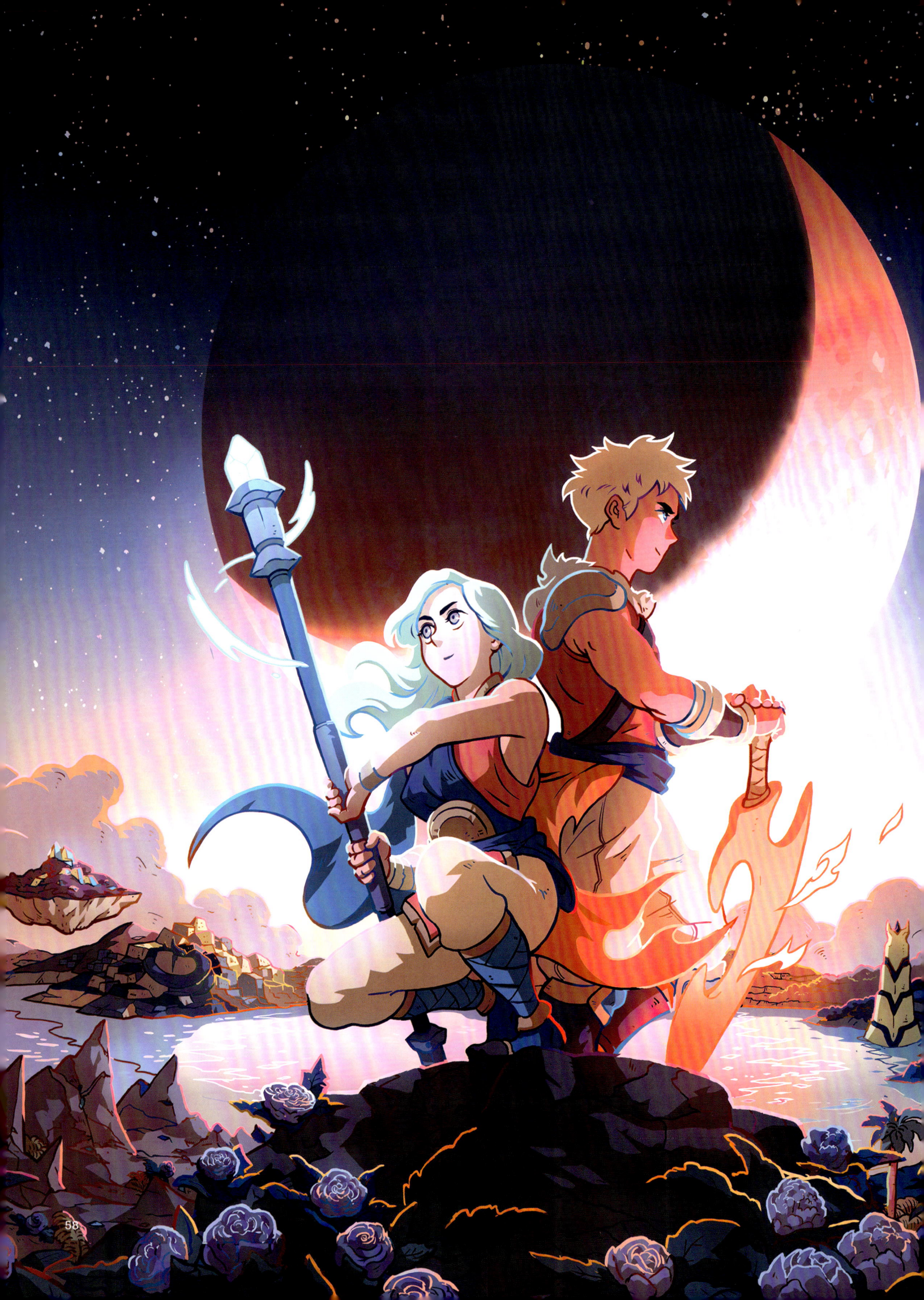

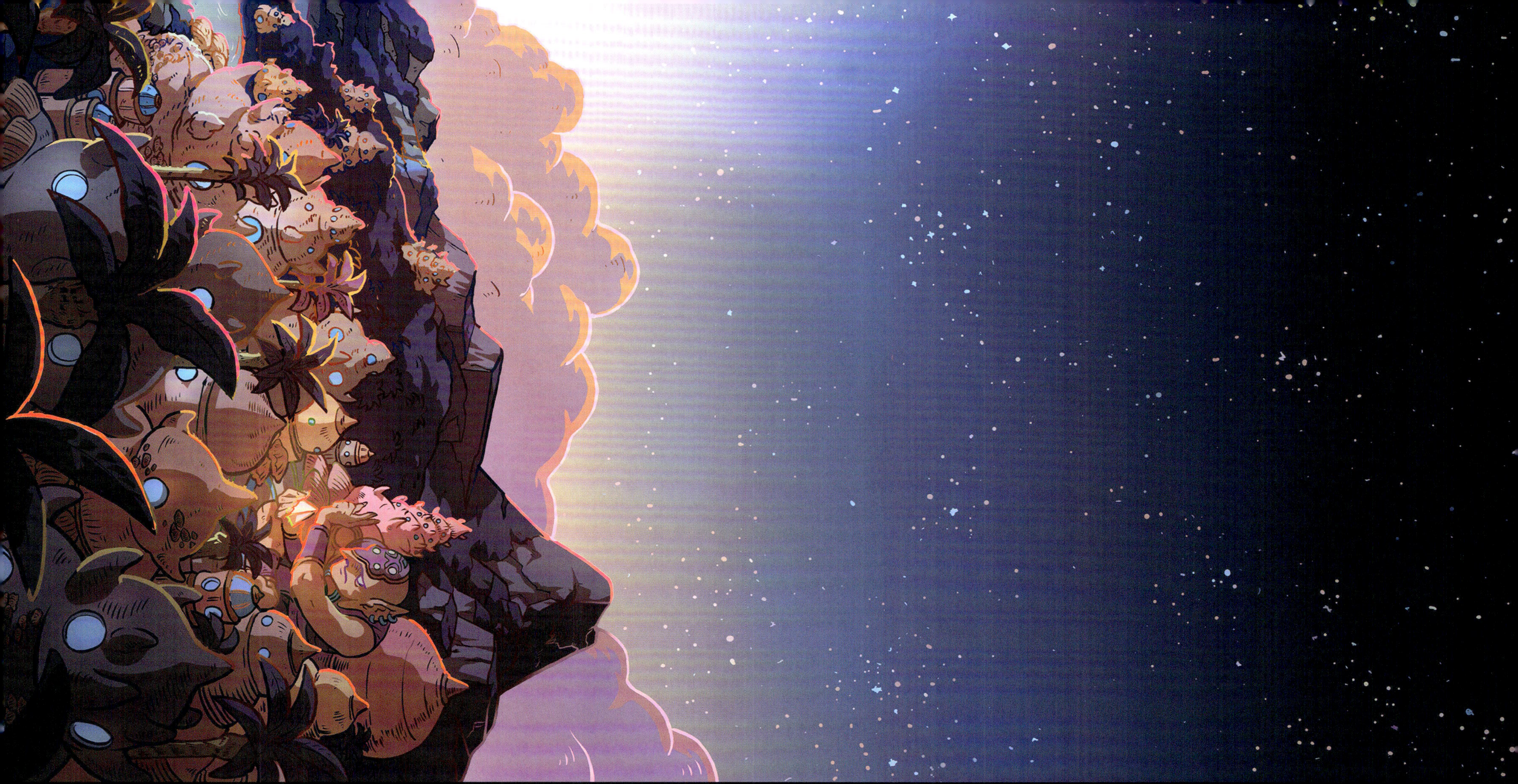

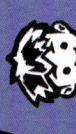

Halo Halo – DLC Art Book Cover

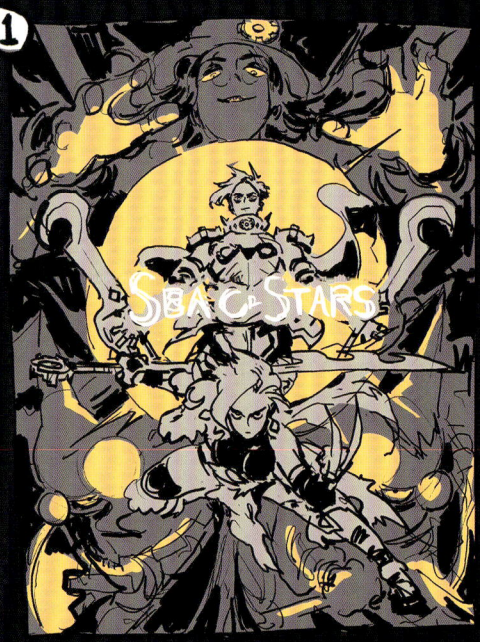
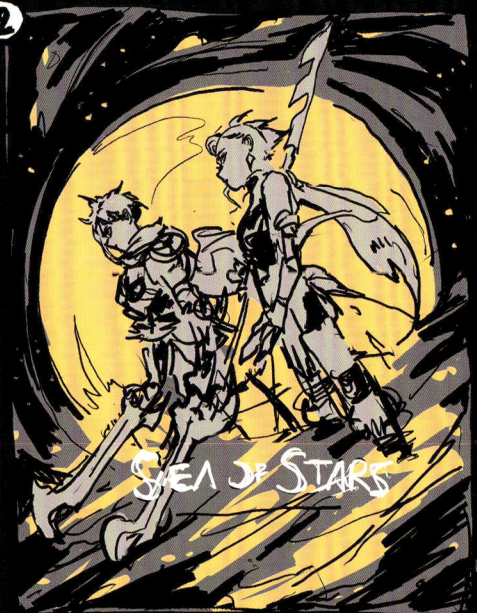
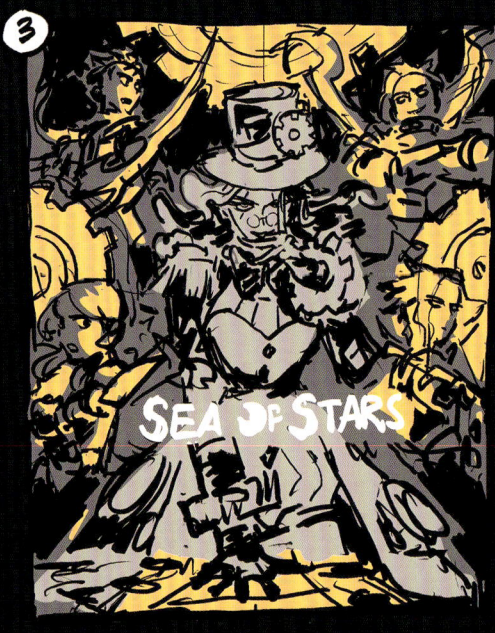

BRYCE: 1. Solstice Heroes Redux – An homage to the first art-book cover, but with their clock-world counterparts. I spent the longest drawing this, so the draftsmanship is the best, lol. I like that this one is very different from the key art for *Throes*. My plan for colour is to go for something very different from the original art-book cover, maybe leaning into reds instead of blues to match the circus vibe.

2. Moon Portal – Trying to channel the original key art with the giant moon, but with a much more sinister vibe. Probably a red moon or maybe even just a crazy energy portal behind them to imply the alternate dimension while still leaning into the franchise's star-themed imagery. Colours might be more like the recent *Equinox* update as well.

3. Versus – Putting the evil Watchmaker front and centre again because she is so cool, lol. The gold-foil treatment is inverted with cogs on the sides and on the Wheels game on the bottom. Kind of a Marvel vs Capcom vibe with the main duos facing off. The most similar to the recent key art, which might make it more on-brand if you guys need to use it for other promo materials as well.

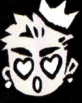

THIERRY: Oof, they're all really strong. I'll sleep on them and share some more detailed feels, but in case it helps, my gut reaction was that #2 is insanely badass, especially picturing someone who knows the heroes but hasn't fully followed. I like the: 'WTF is this dark version of them?'

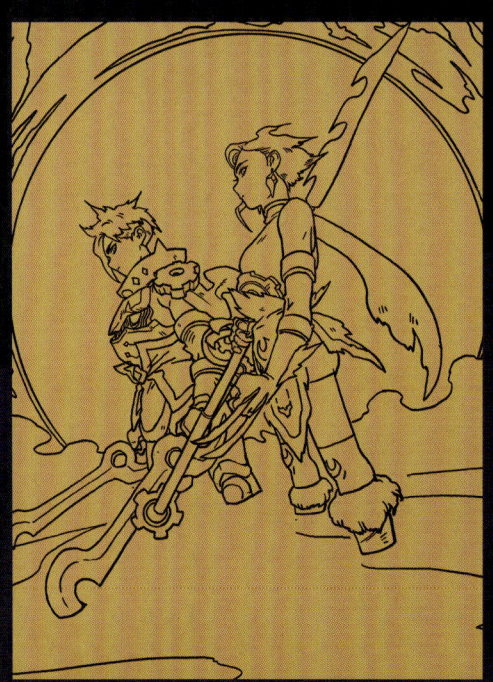
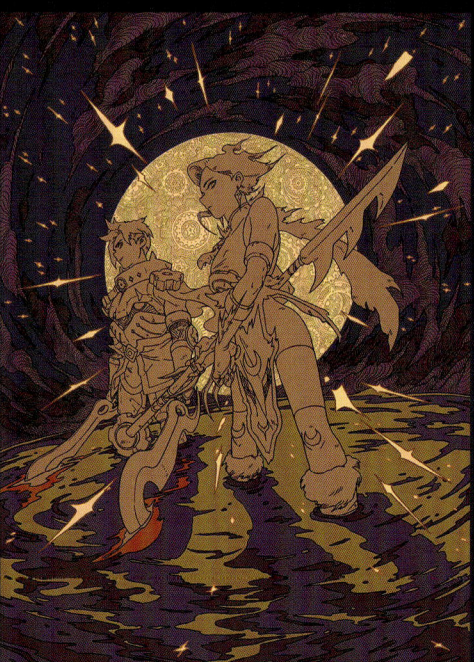
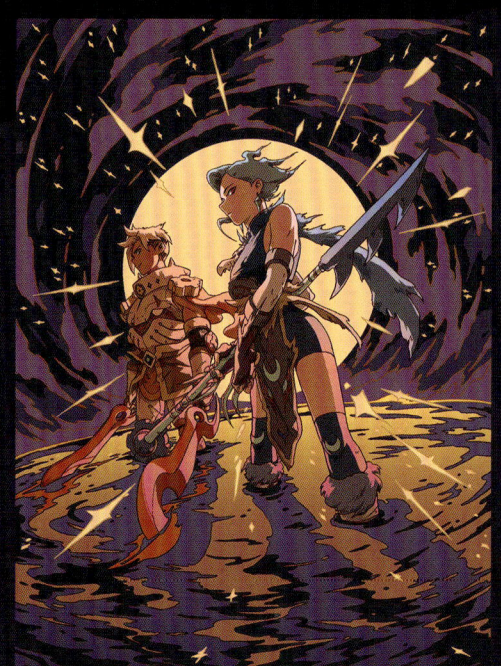

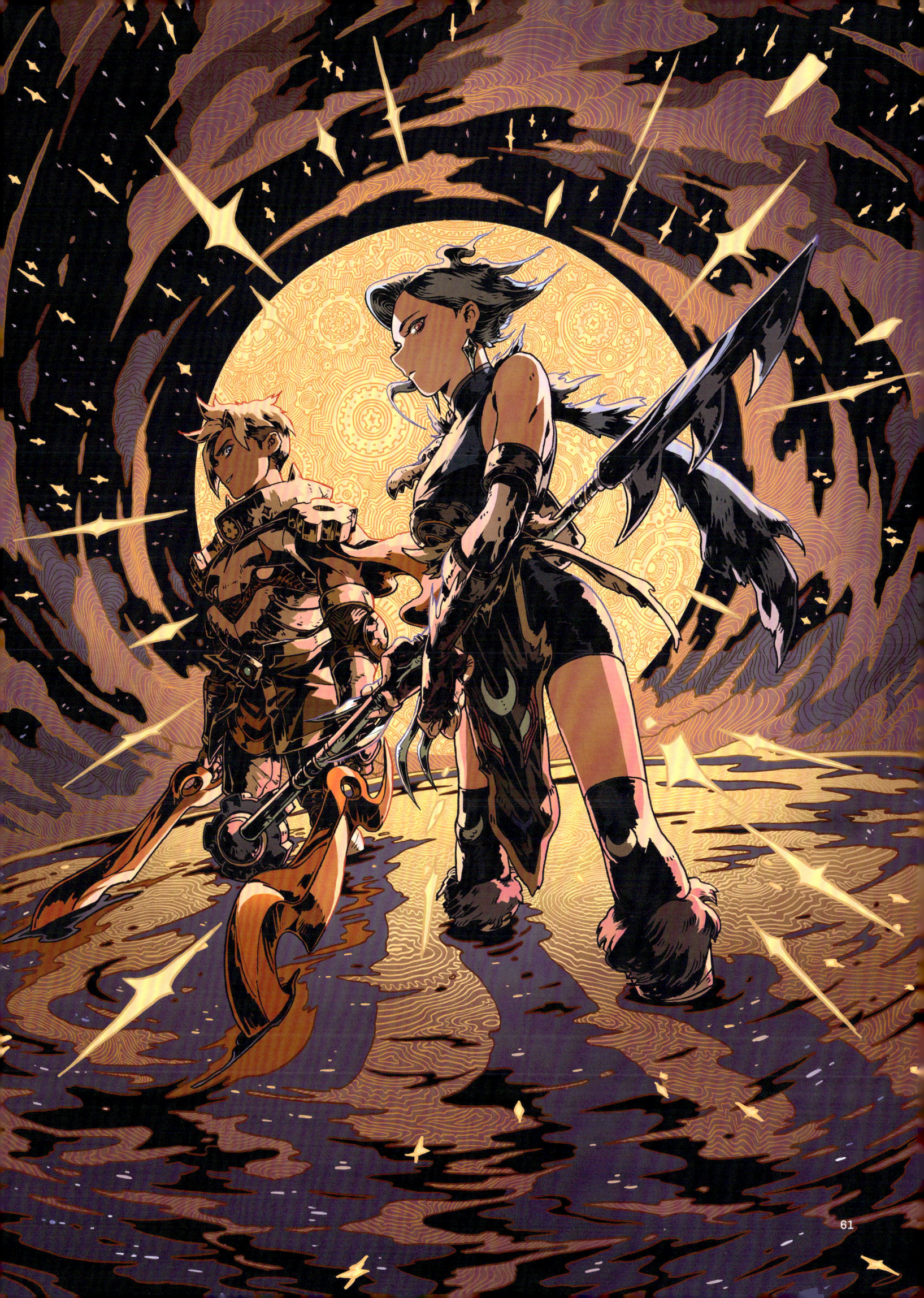

Solar – Sea of Stars Art Book Cover

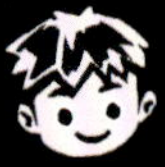

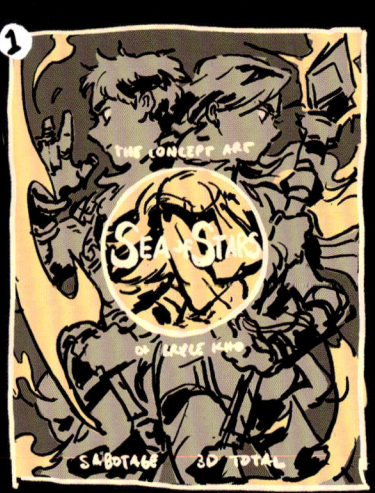

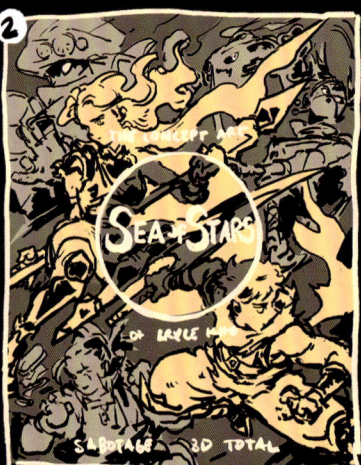

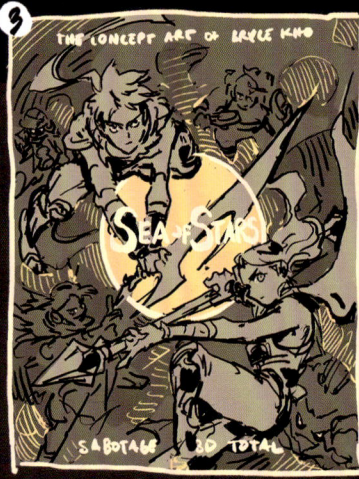

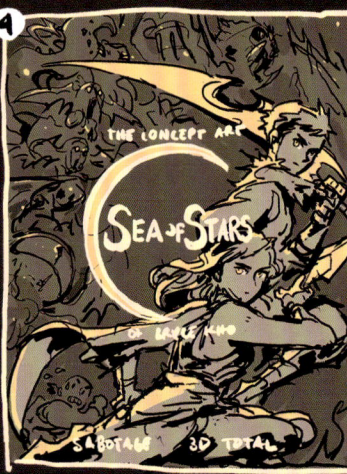

BRYCE: 1. Power Duo – The intent here was to make the gold foil as flashy as possible with a focus on making the weapons' powers pop out. From afar (or as thumbnails on a website), I think the large characters might read most easily, which could help grab viewers. I could also use elements of some of the other options to fill in the background, but probably to a lesser extent given their scale.

2. Solstice Warriors – Purposefully reusing some similar posing from the original concepts I did for the two main characters, as that might remind audiences they've 'seen this before' and pique their interests. The two characters don't have to be entirely gold foil, but the idea is that the circle inverses the gold foil on them so that the book title can pop.

3. Circle Squad – My wife really liked #2's more full-bodied poses, since it evoked 'game concept art' the most. This option is somewhat of an alternative version of that vibe, but with more of an intention for the characters to follow the circle motif. The gold foil here is more of a graphic-design element, playing with the line work that fills in the negative space. Maybe worth mentioning that this effect could work as an alternative foil scheme for pretty much any of the other designs.

4. Eclipse – The only design where the title organically made sense to do in gold foil because the circle was turned into an eclipse. The foil follows a similar 'hair light' function on the characters. In the background, we have the major enemies. The enemies chasing after the heroes is also a callback to the artwork I did for *The Messenger*, which Sabotage fans might notice.

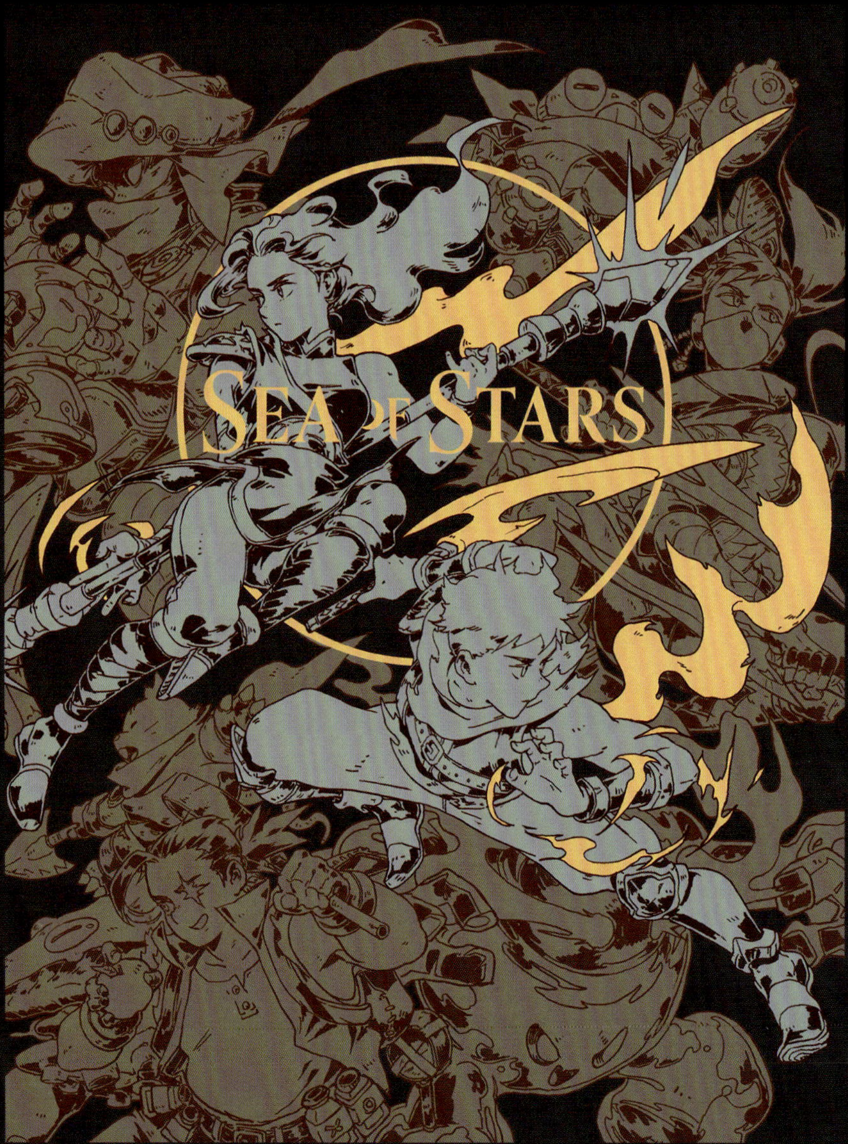

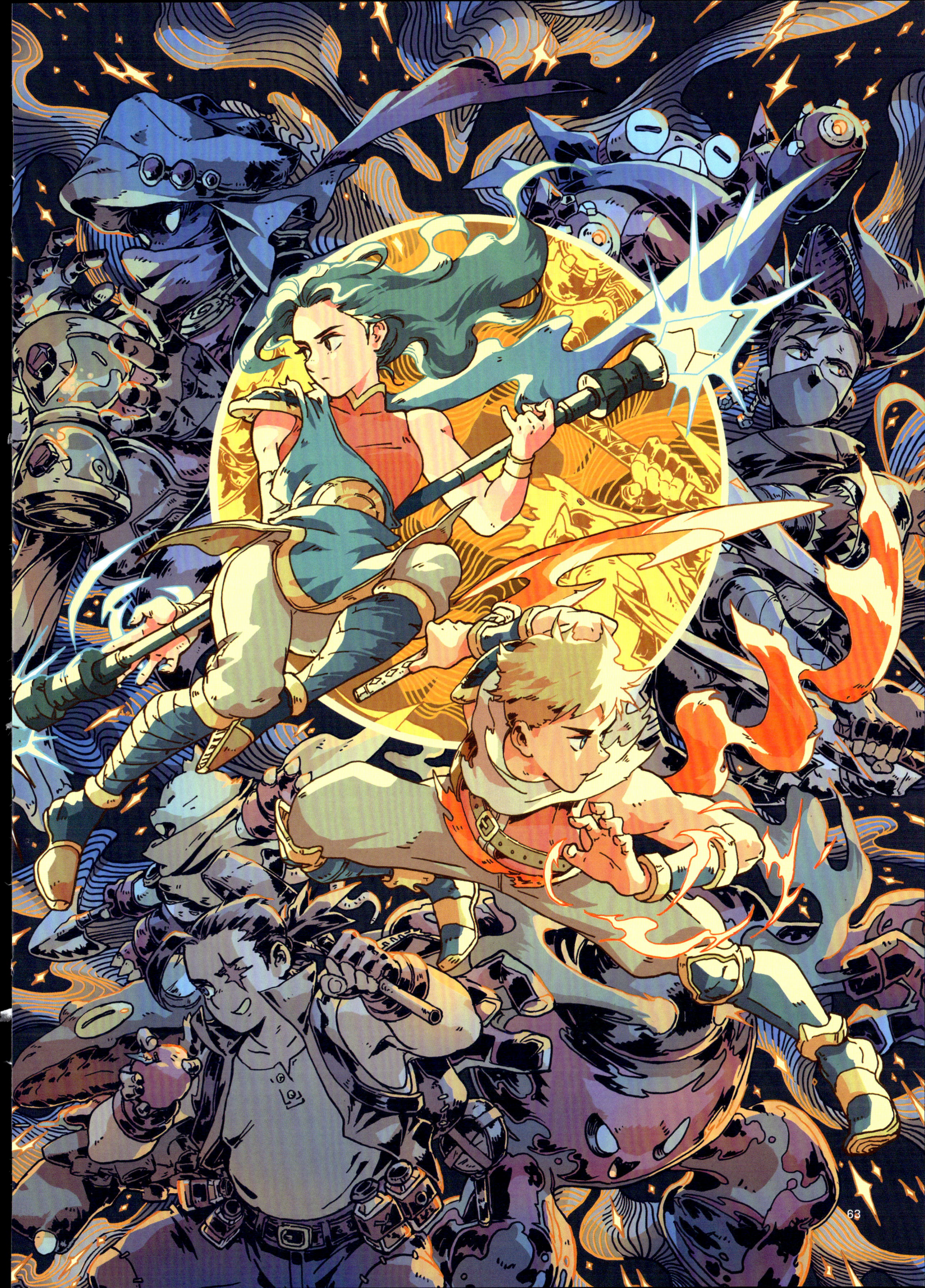

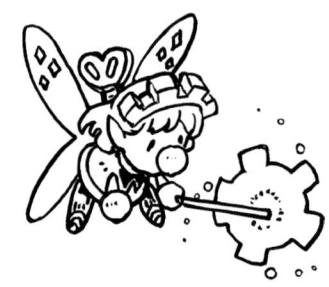

3dtotal Publishing

3dtotal Publishing is a trailblazing, creative publisher specializing in inspirational and educational resources for artists.

Our titles feature top industry professionals from around the globe who share their experience in skillfully written step-by-step tutorials and fascinating, detailed guides. Illustrated throughout with stunning artwork, these best-selling publications offer creative insight, expert advice, and essential motivation. Fans of digital art will enjoy our comprehensive volumes covering Adobe Photoshop, Procreate, and Blender, as well as our superb titles based around character design, including *Fundamentals of Character Design* and *Creating Characters for the Entertainment Industry*. The dedicated, high-quality blend of instruction and inspiration also extends to traditional art. Titles covering a range of techniques, genres, and abilities allow your creativity to flourish while building essential skills.

Well-established within the industry, we now offer over 100 titles and counting, many of which have been translated into multiple languages around the world. With something for every artist, we are proud to say that our books offer the 3dtotal package:

LEARN • CREATE • SHARE

Visit us at store.3dtotal.com

3dtotal Publishing is part of 3dtotal.com, a leading website for CG artists founded by Tom Greenway in 1999.

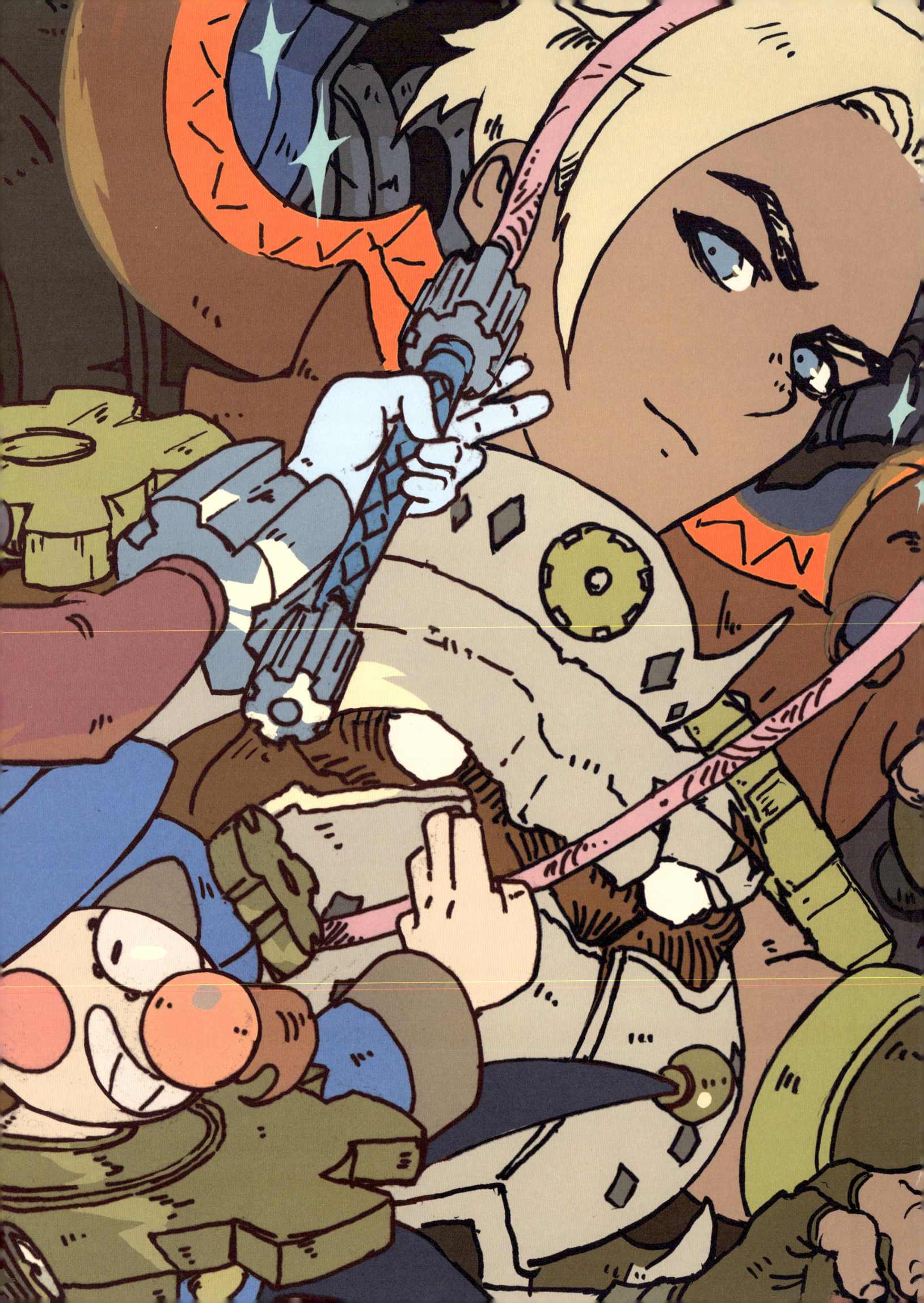